ARMY@LOVE

RICK VEITCH
Writer and Penciller

GARY ERSKINE
Inker

BRIAN MILLER
Colorist

TRAVIS LANHAM
Letterer

ARMY@LOVE CREATED BY RICK VEITCH

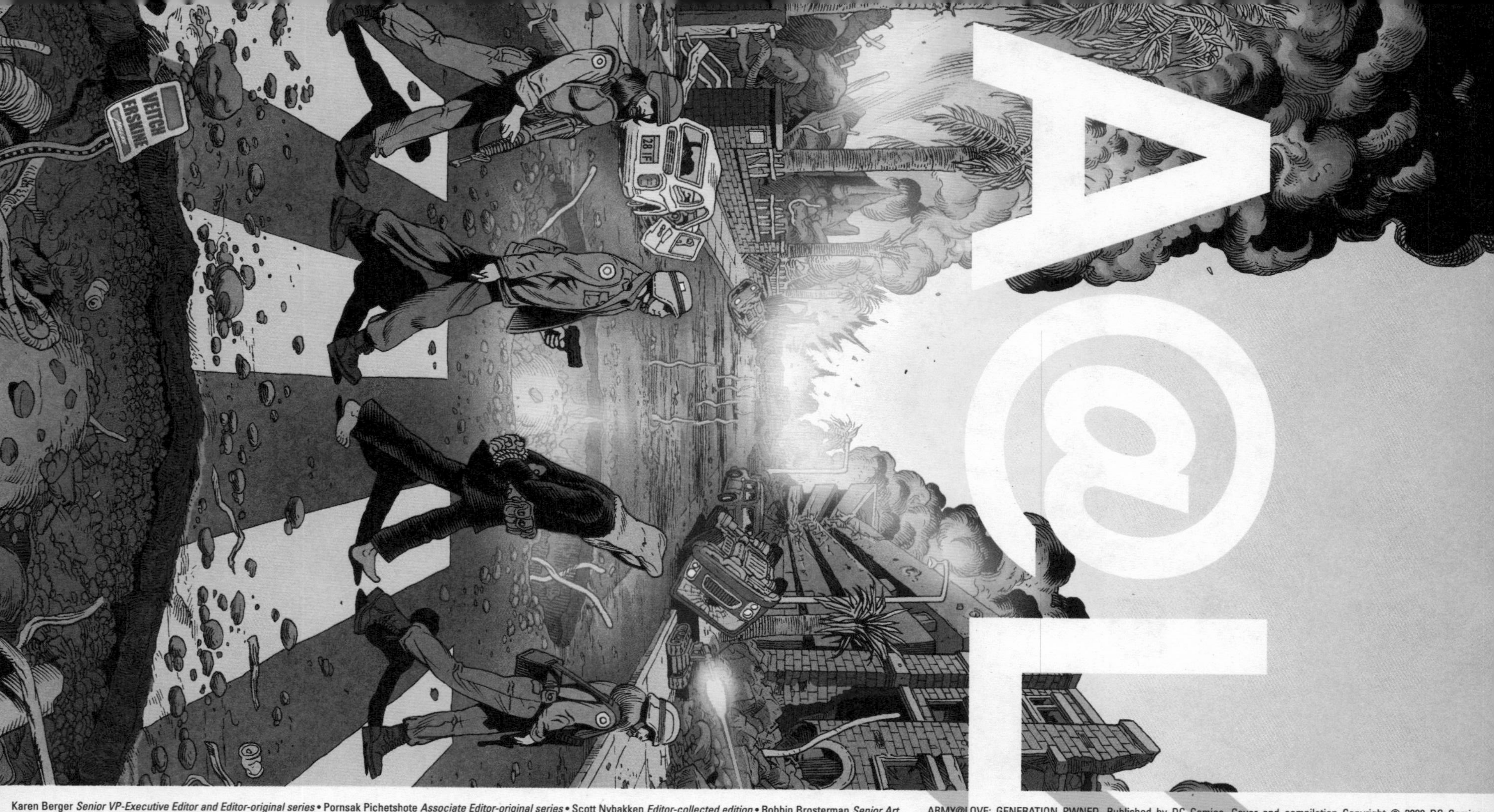

Cover illustration by Rick Veitch and Gary Erskine. Cover color by Brian Miller. Publication design by BrainchildStudios/NYC

DC COMICS 1700 Broadway, New York, NY 10019 A Warner Bros. Entertainment Company.
Printed in Canada. First Printing. ISBN: 978-1-4012-1832-4

ARMY@LOVE V2.0 SPECIFICATIONS

A@L PERSONNEL FILES

THE FRONT LINES

SWITZER
Good girl gone wild.
Answers to: Sgt. Morse
Married to: Loman
Sleeping with: Flabbergast

FLABBERGAST
Stage magician and lothario.
Answers to: Sgt. Morse
Sleeping with: Switzer

MORSE
Old school non-com.
In charge of: Beau Gest, Flabbergast and Switzer

BEAU GEST
Robotic Control specialist 1 class, with Down's syndro
In charge of: Roy the Robo

THE HOME FRONT

LOMAN
Hometown bagman.
Married to: Switzer
Sleeping with: Allie

ALLIE
Lost, lonely, and on a fast plane to nowhere.
Married to: Healey
Sleeping with: Loman

DEE DEE GEST
Never met a system she couldn't work.
Mother of: Beau Gest
Sister of: Loman

BLANCHE
Muscle of Edgefield hot car r
Answers to: Needhawk

MOTIVATION AND MORALE

HEALEY
Head honcho of Motivation and Morale.
Married to: Allie
Answers to: Stelaphane

MAGOON
Creative Consultant for MoMo.
Answers to: Healey

WOYNER
Healey's hyper-efficient secretary.
Answers to: Healey

CABINET

STELAPHANE
Secretary of War with strange collecting habits.
In charge of: Healey and Frick

CLASSIFIED
Office of Motivation and Morale

OY THE ROBOT
dvanced Attack Mobile Weapons
nd Surveillance Platform.
nswers to: Beau Gest
ying on: Switzer and
abbergast

ROYDEN
In love with monsters since he saw his first horror movie.
Answers to: Sgt. Morse
Sleeping with: Anyone he can

NEEDHAWK
Brains of Edgefield hot car ring.
Answers to: Peebles

PEEBLES
Wants to put all of Afbaghistan in the driver's seat.
Answers to: The Almighty Dollar

POMONA PEEBLES
Chip off the old block.
Sleeping with: Not picky
Answers to: Her father

WAR ZONE

FRICK
Stelaphane's Wiccan Chief of Staff.
Answers to: Stelaphane

MAI MAU
Reads every issue of Popular Mechanicals.

JENAN
War widow with designs on Healey.
Answers to: Mai Mau

MICHI
Thirteen going on twenty.
Answers to: Mai Mau and Jenan

MOTIVATION
HOT ZONE
MORALE
Polka Cola
75
2.00

Forward operating base Habitrail, Babel Province, Afbaghistan.
We'll be settin' out for heaven in my little speed boat...

A few years in the future.
There you have it. The stunned crowds in Central Park spontaneously breaking into song...

The heartbroken throngs joining in Paco Lipsync's monster hit which continues to be the number one ring tone in the nation.

A song now forever immortalized after the band's tragic demise yesterday in Afbaghistan...

Four young musical geniuses, murdered while leaving a fundraising concert they'd just performed to benefit war orphans...

Leaving us all with a final indelible reminder of exactly why we are fighting this...
Click

LAAADIES AND GENTLEMEN...
TONIGHT, FOR YOUR EDIFICATION AND AMUSEMENT, WE BRING YOU THE MAGIC TEAM THAT HAS THRILLED AND MESMERIZED THE LOST KINGDOMS OF ASIA!

THE *AMAZING FLABBERGAST* AND *SWITZER!*
...UMMM, *SWITZER* AND THE *AMAZING FLABBERGAST!*

NO! THE *AMAZING SWITZER* AND *FLABBERGAST!* HAHA!
KNOKNOK

YEAH?
HI, HONEY? IT'S ME.
OPEN UP.

BABE? WHAT ARE YOU DOIN' IN THE BAGH?
AHH, IT'S *ALLIE.*

SHE'S BEEN SNATCHED.
OR SOMETHIN'...

SIR, BIG FINGER'S CLOCKING A MONGROLIAN MIG RISING TO INTERCEPT.

HMMF! THEIR RADAR'S FAR TOO PRIMITIVE TO PAINT US. SOME YAK HERDER MUST HAVE CALLED IN A VISUAL.

LOVE IN THE AGE OF INFORMATION

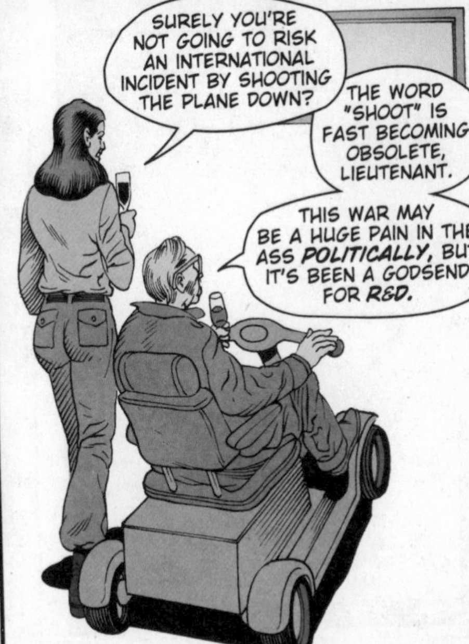

WE'VE GOT SOME LOVELY STUFF IN THE TESTING STAGE.
WELCOME TO THE AUTOMATED COMBAT SUPPORT SYSTEM. PLEASE WAIT WHILE WE CHECK YOUR RETINAL SCAN.
WELCOME, **SECRETARY STELAPHANE.** YOU HAVE ACCESS TO ALL ASSETS.

DO YOU WISH TO TAKE CARE OF THAT APPROACHING BOGEY?
"YES. BUT IT NEEDS TO LOOK LIKE AN ACCIDENT."
THE INTER-ORBITAL ASSASSINATION ARRAY IS AVAILABLE.
"LET'S TRY THAT MICRO-REFRIGERATION LASER."
EXCELLENT CHOICE.
I'M TARGETING THE PILOT'S BRAIN. FLASH-FREEZING THE PRECISE NEURONS THA CONTROL MOVEMENT OF HIS WRISTS.

FORCING HIM TO PUSH DOWN ON THE STICK.
"YOU KNOW WHAT I LIKE ABOUT THIS? IN MINUTES OF THE CRASH, THE VICTIM'S BRAIN CELLS RETURN TO THE AMBIENT TEMPERATURE."

SO THE SYSTEM IS COMPLETELY UNDETECTABLE! HAHA!
AMAZING, SIR.
WITH TECHNOLOGY LIKE ***THIS***, WE CAN COUNTER INSURGENCY ACTIVITY WITHOUT HAVING TO RISK GROUND COMBAT OPERATIONS!
AH! IF ONLY WE HAD THE MONEY!
I TELL YOU, ITS HELLISH HOW WE HAVE TO GROVEL TO BUSINESSMEN TO GET ANYTHING DONE IN THIS WAR!
WE'RE ALMOST OVER THE ***DROP AREA***, SIR.

SINCE THIS WAS YOUR IDEA, I THINK IT'S ONLY FAIR THAT YOU DO THE HONORS, LIEUTENANT.
IT'S THE BIG RED BUTTON. BE SURE TO STAND CLEAR WHEN YOU PUSH IT.
THANK YOU, MAJOR.

HELLO, ALLIE. IT'S ME-- LIEUTENANT WOYNER. REMEMBER?
Y-YES. MY HUSBAND'S SECRETARY CHIEF OF STAFF!
IS HE HERE?

NO.
HE'S... INDISPOSED.
WHILE YOU ARE ABOUT TO BE DISPOSED OF.

WH--WHAT ARE YOU SAYING?
THE COLONEL IS FAR TOO IMPORTANT TO THE WAR EFFORT TO SUFFER ANY MORE OF YOUR HYSTERICS, ALLIE.
WAIT, I GET IT! YOU WANT HIM FOR YOURSELF! THAT'S IT, ISN'T IT?
COLONEL HEALEY MIGHT VERY WELL GO DOWN IN HISTORY AS THE PERSON WHO SAVED OUR COUNTRY, ALLIE.

IS IT WRONG TO GIVE SUCH A TRULY GREAT MAN THE COMFORT HE DESERVES?

POF
SKWWMMMOOF
YOU FUCKING--

SLUUUUUUUUUUUU
UUUUUUUUU
WHOOOMMP
UT!!
PUTT PUTT PUTT
Aa--Hnnh. Ah--Hunh.
Aa--Hnnh. Aah--Hunh.
POF
POF
POF
POF
OOOF!!
PUTT PUTT PUTT
WAIT! WAIT!
COME BACK!

NOT FAIR!
NOT FAIR!
NOT FAIR!
NOT...?
HELLO? I'M...I'M STRANDED, I...
DO YOU HAVE A PHONE? YOU KNOW? TALK TALK?
PHONE THIS WAY? OKAY.
I GUESS...
DO YOU GET GOOD COVERAGE OUT HERE?

SO I SHOULD PROBABLY COVER YOU WHILE YOU HAVE DINNER AND, UH... CONVERSATION WITH JENAN?
JUST A PIT STOP TONIGHT, MAGOON.
I'M UNDER ORDERS FROM STELAPHANE TO PICK UP MY OLD PHONE.

CHECK OUT ALL THESE CARS AND DELIVERY TRUCKS PARKED AT JENAN'S.
HMM. YEAH, THAT'S FUNNY. AND NO KIDS BEGGING FOR TREATS?

AHA! THERE'S MY LITTLE GANG OF ISLAMO-FASCISTS!
HEY--WHO'S LOOKING FOR A CHESTERFIELD CHEW?
BABEEPBOOP

YOU CAN FREEZE IT, CRACK IT OR JUST UNWRAP IT!
HELLO? ANYONE?
BEEPTING ZAP BONG

THEY'RE ACTING LIKE REAL AMERICAN CHILDREN SINCE WE BOUGHT THEM THE GAME BOYS, COLONEL HEALEY!
HEY, JENAN. YOU LOOK... AMAZING. I JUST CAME FOR MY, UH...
MY, UH...
CARE FOR A CANDY BAR?

YOUR TIMING IS RFECT! WE'RE ENOVATING AND CELEBRATING LL AT ONCE!
WHAT DO YOU THINK OF THE NEW COLOR? I'VE GOT ALL MATCHING FURNITURE COMING TOMORROW.
IT TOTALLY CHANGES THE FENG SHUI IN HERE. MUST BE EXPENSIVE THOUGH?

WE'VE, UMMM...HAD A BIT OF LUCK! YOU SEE, MY UNCLE WAS KILLED IN A, UH...BOMBING AND LEFT US A SIZABLE INHERITANCE.
COME OUT ON THE PATIO AND I'LL TELL YOU ALL ABOUT IT.
I'D LOVE TO. IT'S JUST... I CAN'T REALLY STICK AROUND.

SEE, I PROBABLY SHOULD HAVE ASKED YOU FIRST, BUT A COUPLE WEEKS AGO I GAVE MICHI MY OLD CELL PHONE.
NOW IT TURNS OUT I SHOULDN'T HAVE DONE THAT FOR SECURITY REASONS...
MUST WE WORRY OURSELVES WITH SUCH TRIVIAL THINGS? LIFE IS TO BE LIVED.

SAVORED.
IS IT NOT?

THIS IS NO TIME FOR FLIRTING! DON'T YOU UNDERSTAND...?
I'VE GOT TO HAVE THAT PHONE!!

GET YOUR HANDS OFF MY DAUGHTER!
BY GOD, I'LL WHIP YOUR FILTHY BACKSIDE!
MAI MAU-- Haha. I'M SORRY... I DIDN'T MEAN TO... IT'S JUST... Haha...

AGGH! PLEASE. Owtch! I MUST GET THE PHONE BACK! Owtch IT'S ABSOLUTELY IMPERATIVE Owtch!
THAT'S ALL YOU THINK OF-- YOUR CONSUMER TRINKETS!
TOOLS OF SATAN, I SAY!
WHAK
WHAK
WHAK

HERE! I TOOK A HAMMER TO YOUR CURSED PHONE.
WE DON'T WANT YOUR POISON IN OUR HOUSE!
TH-THAT'S IT? Y-YOU'RE SURE IT'S MINE?

AFTER ALL YOU'VE DONE TO JENAN-- NOW YOU CALL ME A LIAR!
WHAK
WHAK
WHAK
NO-- Owtch-- IT'S JUST... Owtch
GET OUT! OUT!

I THOUGHT YOU SOLD HIS PHONE. I MEAN-- THAT'S WHERE ALL THIS MONEY CAME FROM, RIGHT?
PART OF THE DEAL WAS THE NORTH KOREENIANS PROVIDED A KNOCK-OFF WITH COUNTERFEIT SERIAL NUMBERS.

SMASHED INTO BITS, HE WON'T BE ABLE TO TELL THE DIFFERENCE.
BUBEEPBEEPBOOP

EDGEFIELD, NEW JERSEY.
SO NEEDHAWK AND BLANCH DIDN'T COME OUT SO GOOD IN THE FIRE. THEY'RE GONNA TAKE THE FALL.
LOMAN PONIED UP EVERYTHING WE SUSPECTED HIM OF SKIMMING.
THE GUY IS A FUCKING WEASEL.

THIS KIND OF SHIT ALWAYS GOES ON WITH LOMAN.
WE SHOULD TAKE CARE OF HIM ONCE AND FOR ALL.
COPS ARE WORKING WITH US ON THIS TO KEEP IT ALL QUIET. SO I'M GONNA LET IT SLIDE.

IF HE SHOWS UP HERE IN THE BAGH, I'VE GOT FRIENDS WHO KNOW HOW TO MAKE HIM DISAPPEAR.
NOW, PRINCESS-- BE NICE! YOUR FATHER HAS GIVEN HIS WORD.
SO HOW'S THE INVENTORY MOVIN'?

STUFF'S BLOWING IT THE DOORS. BUT MANY BAGHIS ARE STRUNG OUT ON CREDIT.
WE MIGHT HAVE TO WORK WITH THE LOCAL MILITIA TO COLLECT SOME OF IT.
SPEAK OF THE DEVIL...

HERE COMES A FAMILY THAT JUST YESTERDAY SIGNED A NOTE FOR FORTY GRAND.
THEY DROVE OFF THE LOT IN ONE OF OUR EDGEFIELD SPECIALS AND NOW THEY'RE WALKIN' WOUNDED. I BETTER GET OFF.

SO THE CAR ACTUALLY SAVED OUR LIVES WHEN IT STALLED UP THE STREET FROM WHERE THE BOMBER DETONATED HIMSELF.
BUT THE EXPLOSION DESTROYED OUR BUSINESS. AND THE CAR IS A TOTAL LOSS.
UNFORTUNATE. BUT UNDER THE TERMS OF THE CONTRACT, THE LOAN WILL HAVE TO BE REPAID *IMMEDIATELY* OR WE FORECLOSE ON YOUR HOME.

THIS IS EVERY DINAR WE HAVE. THE REST OF THE DEBT WILL BE SETTLED BY MY SON, *ISSA.*
I SERIOUSLY DOUBT THIS DWEEB HAS EVER WORKED A DAY IN HIS LIFE.
MY TRUE CALLING IS *SPIRITUAL,* MA'M.

HAH! SO WHAT ARE YOU GOING TO DO--*PRAY* FOR ME?
I GOT NEWS FOR YOU, KID--ITS WAY TOO LATE FOR *POMONA PEEBLES* IN THE REDEMPTION DEPARTMENT!

ISSA HAS SOME TRAINING IN THE ART OF HOUSEHOLD SERVICE.

I OFFER THE TRADITIONAL AFBAGHI PAYMENT FOR DEBT. FOR ONE FULL YEAR, MY SON WILL ATTEND YOUR EVERY WISH.

YOU MEAN... THE KID'D BE LIKE MY *SERVANT?* WAIT ON ME HAND AND FOOT?

YES, MS. *PEEBLES.*

HAHAHA! WELL, GODDAMMIT!

WHY THE HELL *NOT?*

MAY YOU HONORABLY FULFILL YOUR DUTY IN THE SPIRIT OF GOD, ***ISSA.***

I--I WILL, FATHER. BE BLESSED IN MY ABSENCE.

WILL YOU HURRY IT UP? I GOT A WEEK'S KICKBACK BURNING A HOLE IN MY PURSE!

ASK THEM TO HOLD MY PLACE AT THE SEMINARY.
WE WILL!
SO WHAT'S THE DEAL? YOU'RE BIG TIME INTO THIS RELIGION THING?

YES. I HOPE TO SOMEDAY BE A MINISTER IN THE ZEROMOSTELIAN FAITH. I WANT TO SPREAD THE WORD OF GOD AMONG ALL PEOPLES.
THEN LET'S GET ONE THING ABSOLUTELY FUCKING STRAIGHT FROM THE GIT GO...

I DON'T EVER WANT TO HEAR ANY OF THAT SANCTIMONIOUS BULLSHIT DIRECTED MY WAY.
I LIVE MY OWN LIFE-- I DO WHAT I WANT WITH WHO I WANT. UNDERSTAND?
WE ARE TAUGHT IT IS UNWISE TO WASTE GOD'S SEED BY PLANTING IT IN BARREN EARTH.

RIGHT. SO, YOU GET MANY GIRLFRIENDS IN DIVINITY SCHOOL?
OH NO, MA'AM. MEN AND WOMEN ARE STRICTLY SEGREGATED IN OUR CULTURE.
ALL THOUGHT OF INTIMATE CONTACT WITH THE OPPOSITE SEX IS BANISHED FROM THE MIND UNTIL MATRIMONY.

SOUNDS REPRESSED.
YOU TAKE A LOT OF COLD BATHS?
Victoria's Regrets
I, UH...

I'M LOOKING FOR SOMETHING TO CATCH THE FANCY OF A CERTAIN WELL-SEASONED GENTLEMAN.
We'll be settin' out for heaven in my little speed boat...
HERE'S THE HORNY OLD COOT NOW!
...UH...

HELLOOOO. YOU'RE STILL COMING OVER TONIGHT, I HOPE? OH, GOOOOOD.
YES, IN FACT, I'M AT VICTORIA'S REGRETS RIGHT NOW. YOU WANT TO HELP ME PICK SOMETHING OUT?

THE RED TEDDY IS QUIIIITE ENTICING.
YOU WANT TO SEE ME IN IT?
I THINK THAT CAN BE ARRANGED...
SALE
$99

YOU'LL NEVVVER GUESS WHAT I GOT TODAY.
NOT A GULFSTREAM. HAHA! THAT'S WHAT I WANT FROM YOU!
NO-- I NOW HAVE MY VERY OWN PERSONAL SERVANT.

SO WHAT DO YOU THINK?
I'M GOING TO HOLD YOU TO THAT! HAHAHA

AND THE BEST PART ABOUT THIS SERVANT DEAL? I PUT IT TOGETHER ALL BY MYSELF!
YES. DADDY DIDN'T HAVE TO PULL A SINGLE STRING.

WELL, AT LEAST THEY LET YOU PULL GUARD DUTY.

YEAH. AT THE HOT WASTE RECYCLING FACILITY.

NEXT I'LL BE DOING CARD TRICKS AT THE USO.

IT'S YOUR OWN FAULT, ***FLABB-DUDE.*** YOU LOSE YOUR MOJO IN A FIREFIGHT YOU'RE A DANGER TO THE WHOLE PLATOON.

COMBAT STATUS AIN'T A RIGHT--IT'S A ***PRIVILEGE.***

I KNOW, ***ROYDEN.*** IT'S JUST I GOT IT ***BAD*** THIS TIME.

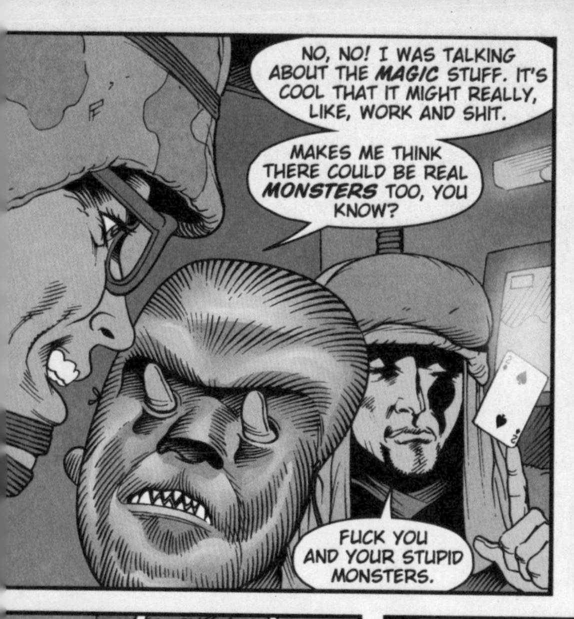
NO, NO! I WAS TALKING ABOUT THE MAGIC STUFF. IT'S COOL THAT IT MIGHT REALLY, LIKE, WORK AND SHIT.
MAKES ME THINK THERE COULD BE REAL MONSTERS TOO, YOU KNOW?
FUCK YOU AND YOUR STUPID MONSTERS.

DUDE--
CHICKS LAUGH AT YOU BECAUSE THEY LIKE YOU. THEY JUST AREN'T READY TO ADMIT IT.
THING TO DO IS MAKE CONTACT. WORK ON HER.
I SHOULD BE FOCUSING ON MY JOB. SOM OF THE STUFF STO HERE WOULD BE DANGEROUS IN TH WRONG HANDS.

THOSE MINI-REACTOR CASINGS ARE SO HOT THEY'LL FRY AN EGG.
YEAH, BUT THE ROBOTS TAKE DOWN ANYTHING THAT MOVES.
GIVE HER A CALL.

THINK I SHOULD?
WHAT HAVE YOU GOT TO LOSE?

SHE'S OFF-DUTY TONIGHT. PROBABLY KICKING BACK IN HER TRAILER.
JUST HOPING SOMEONE'LL GIVE HER A BUZZ, I BET.

YEAH BUT, WHAT IF SHE HAS SOMEONE, Y'KNOW...THERE WITH HER?
GETTIN' IT ON...?

I MEAN, THAT WOULD JUST BE, LIKE, THE WORST THING I CAN IMAGINE.

THIS IS WEIRD.
WHAT? HAVIN' ME HERE?

NO. THAT ALLIE WOULD GET *KIDNAPPED.*
I MEAN, IT HAS TO BE SOMEONE WHO NEVER READ ***"THE RANSOM OF RED CHIEF."***
SHE'S NOT THAT BAD. A LITTLE DEPRESSED, BUT...

SHE'S A WALKING, TALKING BLACK HOLE! I DON'T KNOW WHAT ATTRACTS YOU GUYS TO HER.
I TOLJA'. WITH HER 'N' ME IT WASN'T LIKE REAL ATTRACTION. SHE WAS LONELY. THAT'S ALL.
HEALEY'D NEVER TALK TO HER AND SHIT.

YOU USED TO WORK WITH HIM AT MOMO. WHAT'S HE REALLY LIKE?
HEALEY'S A FLAKE BUT HE GIVES GREAT POWERPOINT...
HE STARTED WITH A LITTLE MARKETING DEPARTMENT THAT SOMEHOW CAUGHT THE EYE OF THE PENTAGON.

HE PITCHED THEM ON CREATIVE WAYS TO SELL THE WAR, THOUGH MOST OF THE IDEAS WERE WOYNER'S.
THE BRASS WAS SO DESPERATE THEY TRIED SOME OF THE THINGS.
LIKE THOSE ADS YOU SEE WITH THE ***SOLDIERS*** IN THEIR ***UNDERWEAR?***

PUTTING WOMEN IN ***COMBAT.*** GIVING US ***PHONES.*** AND THOSE ***RETREATS*** I TOLD YOU ABOUT.
THE THING SEEMS TO HAVE REALLY STRUCK A NERVE. EVERYONE WANTS TO BE IN COMBAT UNIT ALL OF A SUDDEN.
I DON'T...

WELL YOU'RE AN OLD FUDDY-DUDDY.
I'VE HEARD SOME STORIES ABOUT YOU, MISTER LOMAN!
WHADDYA MEAN? WHAT KIND OF STORIES?

THAT YOU ARE A PERVERT WHO WEARS WOMEN'S UNDERWEAR!
AND LOOK--IT'S ALL TRUE!
HEY! HAHA! HOW'D YOU DO THAT?

IT'S THIS MAGICIAN'S COAT. IT'S LOADED WITH SECRET POCKETS FULL OF STUFF. I'M GETTING PRETTY GOOD.
OH YEAH. FROM CASINO NIGHT. WEREN'T YOU GONNA GIVE IT BACK TO THAT GUY?

I HAVEN'T SEEN FLABBERGAST TO RETURN IT.
I MEAN, I'VE SEEN HIM. IT'S JUST...
SOMETHING HAPPENIN' I SHOULD KNOW ABOUT?

THE TRUTH IS HE'S GOT THIS CRAZY CRUSH ON ME. BUT IT'S LIKE, ARTIFICIAL.
I'M TRYING TO HELP HIM WORK THROUGH IT.
SO YOU SORT OF SEE HIM...REGULAR AND STUFF?

BABE--YOU DIDN'T COME TO THE BAGH JUST TO GET ALL JEALOUS ON ME, DID YOU?
NAAAH. I'M LOOKIN' FOR ALLIE. THAT'S ALL.
THING IS, I MIGHT NEED A PLACE TO STAY WHILE I'M HERE.

WELL. I SUPPOSE YOU CAN CRASH WITH ME. AS LONG AS YOU CAN HANDLE MY LIFESTYLE.
IT'S NOT LIKE BACK HOME HERE.
OKAY. I HEAR YA. JUST LET ME KNOW IF I'M IN THE WAY.
We'll be settin' out for heaven in my little speed boat...
HELLO? OH HIIII! HOW YOU FEELIN'? NO CHANGE, HUH?
OH, NUTHIN'. JUST SITTIN' AROUND.
I WAS THINKING MAYBE YOU SHOULD TALK TO THE PHARMACIST?
HE MIGHT BE ABLE TO GIVE YOU SOMETHING TO, Y'KNOW...DULL THE SPELL?
BABEEPBEEPBOOP
ALLIE
1-555-691-4261
WHAT DO YOU MEAN YOU DON'T THINK YOU'RE UNDER A SPELL?
WE'RE SORRY. THE NUMBER YOU HAVE DIALED IS EITHER OUT OF RANGE OR NO LONGER IN SERVICE.

這是父親

請歡迎我的新妻子

受歡迎的姐妹
I DON'T UNDERSTAND WHAT YOU'RE SAYING, I...

WE ARE SAYING "WELCOME, SISTER."
YOU SPEAK ENGLISH? OH, THANK GOD!

YOU'VE GOT TO HELP ME! I'VE BEEN KIDNAPPED AND...
OF COURSE YOU HAVE.
YOU SOUND LIKE A JERSEY GIRL. I'M FROM NEW HAVEN MYSELF.

NO--YOU DON'T UNDERSTAND. I WAS *REALLY KIDNAPPED!*
WE *ALL* WERE, SISTER.
THAT'S HOW *MONGROLIANS* GET THEIR WIVES.

M-MONGROLIA? IS THAT LIKE SOMEWHERE IN ANTARCTICA?
CENTRAL ASIA.
WELCOME TO YOUR NEW HOME.

WAIT! ***NO!*** LISTEN. I ***MUST*** GET BACK TO CIVILIZATION.
I CAN GET YOU MONEY.
THANK YOU! *HAHAHA!* BUT THERE IS NO USE FOR IT HERE.

BUT I HAVE TO HAVE CERTAIN THINGS! LIKE A ***PHONE*** AND MY ***MEDICATION*** AND...
WHY ARE THEY LAUGHING?
HAHAHA. WHEN ***BATSUKH*** FIRST TOOK US, THAT'S HOW WE EACH REACTED.

YOU'RE NOT ***LISTENING!*** I ALREADY ***HAVE*** A HUSBAND!
HE'S WELL CONNECTED WITH THE UNITED STATES MILITARY AND IS PROBABLY OUT LOOKING FOR ME RIGHT THIS MINUTE!
IN TIME YOU WILL PRAY THAT HE GIVES UP HIS SEARCH.

YOU'LL SEE.

HOT ZONE

BUNGLING BROS. INTERNATIONAL TRAVELING PEACE CIRCUS, DUMBAR PROVINCE, AFBAGHISTAN

OKAY-- HANG THE FUCK UP AND SET THE FUCKING PHONES TO TAKE FUCKING MESSAGES.

I NEED YOUR ***MINDS*** HERE AS WELL AS YOUR ASSES.

SEE! GENGHIS KON
AND HIS PACHYDER
HAREM OF HARLOT

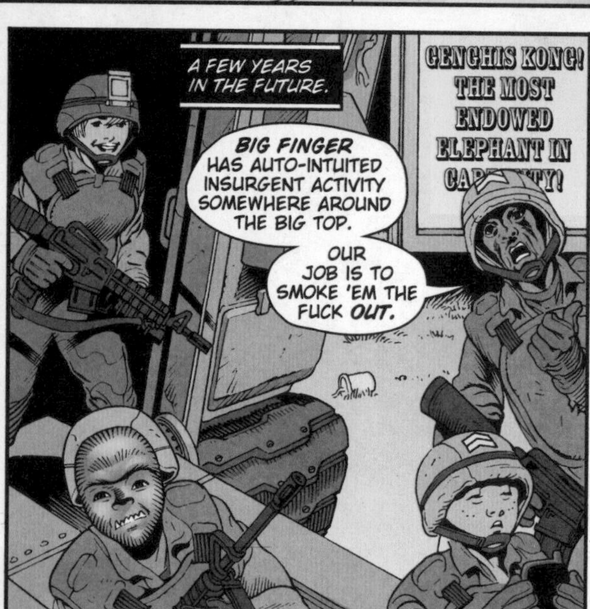

A FEW YEARS IN THE FUTURE.
GENGHIS KONG! THE MOST ENDOWED ELEPHANT IN
BIG FINGER HAS AUTO-INTUITED INSURGENT ACTIVITY SOMEWHERE AROUND THE BIG TOP.
OUR JOB IS TO SMOKE 'EM THE FUCK OUT.

HEY, ROYDEN. WHAT'S WITH FLABBERGAST? IS HE STILL OFF COMBAT STATUS?
HE'S HOPELESS, THAT GUY.
KONG!
PROGENY THAN THE GREAT KHAN!
THANKS TO THE ALLURE OF A CERTA
MISS BUSY-BUNS, I MIGHT ADD.

TAKING DOWN THE UNIT'S TOP PARTY ANIMAL EARNS YOU BRAGGIN' RIGHTS, SWITZER.
DON'T BLAME ME. I DIDN'T PLANT THAT LOVE CHARM ON HIM.
WAIT A SEC--YOU NOTICE HOW THE CROWD'S MOVING?

THEY'RE ALL SHYING AWAY FROM US. NORMAL BEHAVIOR CONSIDERING WE'RE ARMED TO THE TEETH.
BUT THEY'RE ALSO AVOIDING THE ELEPHANT TENT.

MAYBE THERE'S SOMETHING TO THE HERD INSTINCT.

YOU'RE READIN' THOSE TEA-LEAVES RIGHT, SWITZER!
THE PLACE IS CRAWLING WITH HADJ!
AND THEY'RE PLANNIN' MISCHIEF WITH GENGHIS AND HIS STRING OF HONEYS!
THEY MUST BE USING 'EM AS SUPER-SIZE SUICIDE BOMBERS.
NOT IF WE BLOW THE WHOLE PLACE TO BLOODY DIARRHEA.
SLOUCHING TO AFBAGHISTAN
WE CAN'T TARGET ELEPHANTS, ROYDEN! THEY'RE AN ENDANGERED SPECIES!
GOOD POINT.
LET'S ALERT THE REST OF THE UNIT. SARN'T MORSE WILL KNOW HOW TO HANDLE THIS.

THEY'RE GONNA DETONATE SOME FUCKING **DUMBOS?**
I **SWEAR!** IT GETS MORE LIKE A PEE-WEE'S FUCKING PLAYHOUSE AROUND HERE EVERY FUCKING DAY !
Ahem **SERGEANT MORSE?** MAY I HAVE A WORD WITH YOU?

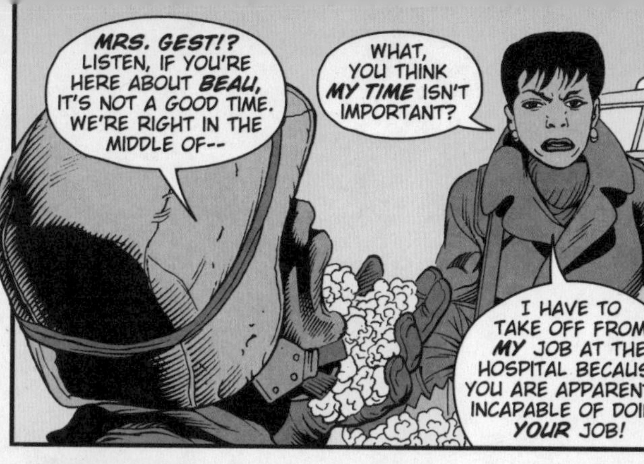
MRS. GEST!? LISTEN, IF YOU'RE HERE ABOUT ***BEAU,*** IT'S NOT A GOOD TIME. WE'RE RIGHT IN THE MIDDLE OF--
WHAT, YOU THINK ***MY TIME*** ISN'T IMPORTANT?
I HAVE TO TAKE OFF FROM ***MY*** JOB AT THE HOSPITAL BECAUS YOU ARE APPAREN INCAPABLE OF DOI ***YOUR*** JOB!

YOU PROMISED MY SON HIS OWN PHONE AND AS OF ***RIGHT NOW*** HE ***STILL*** DOES NOT HAVE IT!
I KNOW! I KNO THERE'S ONE I MY PACK. BUT I GOT A ***SITUATI*** HERE!
IT'S TH ELEPHANT ***MOM.***

WHAT'S THAT, MY BEAUTIFUL BOY? THE SERGEANT WON'T LET YOU SEE THE ***ELEPHANTS*** EITHER?
NO! THE BAD GUYS ARE GOING TO HURT ***GENGHIS KONG*** AND HIS GIRL-FRIENDS!
THE INSURGENTS HAVE THE ANIMALS CORRALLED IN THAT TENT. I'M GONNA CALL IN A DRONE AND TAKE THEM ALL OUT.
NOOOO! NOT THE ELEPHANTS, SARN'T!
GENGHIS I-IS MY FUH-FAVORITE! WAAAA!
JEEZUS ON A SOUPED-UP ***SEGWAY!***

I SUPPOSE I WILL HAVE TO BE THE ONE TO THINK CREATIVELY HERE.
BABYLON GENERAL HOSPITAL. HOW MAY I DIRECT YOUR CALL?
THIS IS ***DEE GEST.***
GIVE ME THE TESTING LAB.

THIS IS NOT PROCEEDING AS PLANNED. STELAPHANE'S PLANE LANDED OVER AN HOUR AGO.
IT'S NOT LIKE WOYNER TO BLOW OFF A MOTIVATION & MORALE MEETING.
SHE'S PROBABLY JUST DOING A LITTLE CAREER CLIMBING.

BLOWING SUNSHINE UP POWERFUL ASSHOLES IS THE SECRET OF SUCCESS.
HEY, YOU OKAY? YOU KEEP WORKING THAT SHOULDER LIKE IT WAS GIVING YOU PROBLEMS.
MAI MAU CAUGHT ME SOME GOOD ONES WITH HER SWITCH. I THINK SHE BROKE THE SKIN IN A COUPLE PLACES.

I'VE GOT SOME ANTISEPTIC COCONUT BUTTER RIGHT HERE.
TAKE OF YOUR SHIRT AND I'LL DAB YOU.
THANKS, MAGOON. DAMN THOUGHTFUL.

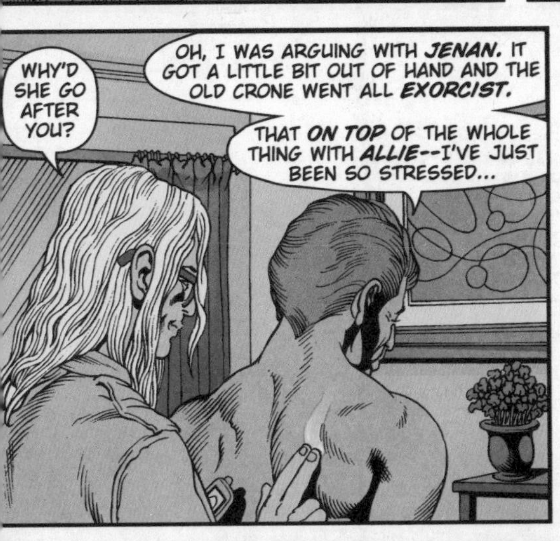
WHY'D SHE GO AFTER YOU?
OH, I WAS ARGUING WITH JENAN. IT GOT A LITTLE BIT OUT OF HAND AND THE OLD CRONE WENT ALL EXORCIST.
THAT ON TOP OF THE WHOLE THING WITH ALLIE--I'VE JUST BEEN SO STRESSED...

WOMEN! THEY'RE NOT WORTH THE TROUBLE SOMETIMES, YOU KNOW WHAT I MEAN?
ALWAYS COOKING UP PLOTS BEHIND YOUR BACK.
YOU GOT THAT RIGHT. OOOH. KEEP THAT UP. RIGHT THERE.

I HOPE I'M NOT INTERRUPTING ANY PLOTS GOING ON BEHIND ANYONE'S BACK.
OH, UH...HEY, WOYNER.
WE, UH... HEHEH... THOUGHT YOU HAD FORGOTTEN THE MEETING.

GOOD THING I DIDN'T. SINCE ***SOME*** JUNIOR-GRADE OFFICERS AROUND HERE WILL DO ***ANYTHING*** TO FURTHER THEIR CAREERS.

AND SOME ***OTHER*** JUNIOR GRADE OFFICERS REALLY SHOULDN'T THROW STONES, SHOULD THEY?

YOU ***ARE*** AWFULY LATE, ***WOYNER.*** WHAT WERE YOU AND ***STELAPHANE,*** UH... DISCUSSING?

I TOOK THE OPPORTUNITY OF MY TIME WITH THE SECRETARY TO MAKE SIGNIFICANT PROGRESS IN SOME IMPORTANT AREAS.

FIRST, HE WANTS TO KNOW IF YOU'VE SUCCESSFULLY RETRIEVED YOUR PHONE FROM ***JENAN'S*** HOUSE?

I HOPE SO. ***MAI MA*** SAID SHE TOO A HAMMER TO IT.

WE'LL HAVE NANO-TECH DO AN AUTOPSY.

IN THE MEANTIME WE CAN'T TAKE ANY CHANCES. ***JENAN'S*** HOUSE WILL HAVE TO BE PUT UNDER SURVEILLANCE.

I GOT A NEW BUG I WANT TO TRY. I'LL GET PLACED IN HER HOUSE.

THE GOOD NEWS IS THE SECRETARY AND I CAME UP WITH A FINAL SOLUTION TO THE ALLIE PROBLEM.
FINAL? YOU MEAN SHE'S--
FINAL IN THAT WE'VE FOUND HER A PERMANENT HOME IN OUTER MONGROLIA WHERE SHE WILL BE VERY HAPPY FOR THE REST OF HER LIFE.

BIG FINGER IS CREATING A DIVORCE COURT JUDGMENT WITH ALL LEGAL DOCUMENTATION AS WE SPEAK.
SHE'S GONE? JUST LIKE... POOF?

YES, COLONEL. THE PROBLEM HAS BEEN SOLVED. YOU'RE FREE.
THAT'S WHAT YOU WANTED, WASN'T IT?
I, UH...GUESS SO. I KNOW OUR RELATIONSHIP'S BEEN DYSFUNCTIONAL, BUT... I MEAN...SHE IS MY WIFE.

HOW COULD SHE BE HAPPY WITHOUT ME?
SHOOT ME NOW.
I AM SOOO TEMPTED.

THIS IS INSANE! ALL I DO IS *KVETCH* ABOUT MY WIFE AND SUDDENLY I'M THE LEADING MAN IN A HITCHCOCK FILM!
WHAT IF WORD GETS OUT? IT COULD UNDERMINE EVERYTHING I'VE DONE WITH *MOTIVATION & MORALE!* BRING DOWN MY WHOLE *CAREER!*
I MEAN-- MOMO'S POSITIONED ME FOR A SENATE SEAT!
STUFF LIKE THIS IS *BOUND* TO BE USED IN ANY ELECTION CAMPAIGN!
THAT'S THE BEAUTY OF SECRETARY *STELAPHANE'S* PERSONAL COMMITMENT, COLONEL.
WHAT COMMITMENT?
HE DELIVERED *ALLIE* TO OUTER MONGROLIA IN HIS OWN PLANE. IT'S HIS GUARANTEE THAT *NOTHING* ABOUT THIS INCIDENT WILL EVER SURFACE ANYWHERE OR ANYTIME.
IF IT DID, IT WOULD TAKE HIM DOWN TOO.
THAT'S DIFFERENT.

BUT I'M STILL ANGRY. AND I HAVE A *RIGHT* TO BE.
YOU'D THINK I'D BE CONSULTED ON MATTERS LIKE THIS, BUT... *Bunhh*
MY PERSONAL GOAL HAS ALWAYS BEEN TO INSURE YOUR SUCCESS, SIR. YOU KNOW THAT.

YOU'RE A T-TREASURE, *WOYNER.*
I--I THINK I COULD USE A LITTLE DOWN TIME.
MAGOON-- I'M GOING TO TAKE THE COLONEL UP TO MY SUITE AND SEE IF I CAN'T HELP HIM RELAX.
WE'LL NEED THAT BUG PLANTED AT *JENAN'S* IMMEDIATELY.
MAYBE YOU COULD WORK ON THAT?
WHY NOT? I KNOW WHEN I'M OUTMANEUVERED.

OKAY, BUG...TIME TO GO TO WORK.
THANK YOU FOR CHOOSING THE FLY ON THE WALL INSECTILE SURVEILLANCE DRONE.
PERFORMING *munchmunch* DNA AUTHORIZATION.

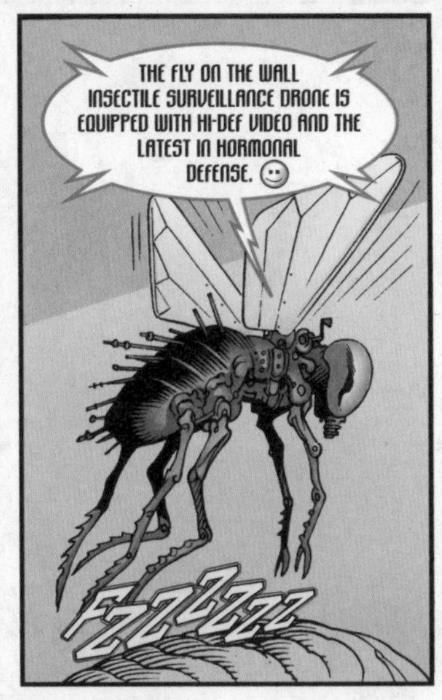
THE FLY ON THE WALL INSECTILE SURVEILLANCE DRONE IS EQUIPPED WITH HI-DEF VIDEO AND THE LATEST IN HORMONAL DEFENSE.
FZZZZZZZ

OKAY, I DON'T NEED ANOTHER AD. YOU GOT YOUR COORDINATES. GO DO YOUR STUFF.
THE FLY ON THE WALL INSECTILE SURVEILLANCE DRONE IS BROUGHT TO YOU BY RADIO-8. KILLS BUGS WHERE THEY LIVE.
FUCK YOU.

HMMM. WAIT A MINUTE. COME BACK HERE.

I'VE GOT SOME NEW COORDINATES FOR YOU.

PERHAPS I HAVEN'T BEEN OUTMANEUVERED AFTER ALL.

SO WHAT ARE WE UP TO?
SUTRA NUMBER ONE HUNDRED AND TWELVE.
"MONKEY CHASING WEASEL"
WE'LL BE SETTIN' OUT FOR HEAVEN IN MY LITTLE SPEED BOAT!

WINTER PASTURE, SINKYANG FRONTIER, OUTER MONGROLIAN REPUBLIC
BREE, WHY IS EVERYONE HERE SUDDENLY ACTING AFRAID OF ME?
BATSUKH'S OTHER WIVES AND CHILDREN AREN'T FAMILIAR WITH EYE-SHADOW, SO THEY ARE WAITING FOR YOU TO DEMONSTRATE YOUR POWERS.
IN MONGROLIA, PEOPLE WHO PAINT THEIR FACES ARE GREAT SHAMANS.
THE ONLY MAGIC ACT I PLAN TO PERFORM IS TO DISAPPEAR.
FORTUNATELY, THE WEASEL SLUT WHO WENT THROUGH MY BAGS MISSED MY SPARE PHONE.
I'VE JUST GOT TO FIND A PLACE WHERE I CAN PICK UP A SIGNAL.
YOU MIGHT GET SOMETHING IN THE HIGH SUMMIT PASTURE. THERE'S A THOUSAND-MILE VIEW ON A CLEAR DAY UP THERE.
JUST DON'T ATTEMPT THE CLIMB ALONE OR UNPREPARED. THE MOTHER OF MOUNTAIN PROWLS THOSE ALTITUDES.
如果_攀登山_必須穿
這件外套為保護
BATSUKH SAYS HE HAS A GIFT FOR HIS NEW WIFE.
TELL HIM I'M NOT HIS WIFE AND I AM QUITE WARM IN MY OWN PARKA. BESIDES-- HIS GIFT SMELLS LIKE A BARN!
OF COURSE! THIS IS A SPECIAL COAT--SOAKED IN MUCH CONSECRATED YAK SPERM.
IT IS THE ONLY THING THAT WILL PROTECT YOU FROM THE SHARP CLAWS OF MOTHER OF MOUNTAIN.
BLEEEE-AGH!
TELL YOUR LORD AND MASTER IT WILL TAKE A LOT MORE THAN RAGS AND GHOST STORIES TO IMPRESS ME.
NOW IF YOU'LL EXCUSE ME, I HAVE TO CALL MY REAL HUSBAND!

BUT NOT MUCH *Huff* BATTERY LEFT.
THERE'S A SIGNAL! IT'S FAINT BUT...

YES! I GOT A SOLID BAR!
AND ANOTHER ONE *Huff* *FLICKERING!*

YES! *Puff* *THREE* BARS!
AND JUST ENOUGH CHARGE FOR ONE CALL! THANK GOD!

GEE, IT *IS* KIND OF... ATMOSPHERIC UP HERE. COULDN'T BE ANYTHING TO THIS *MOTHER OF MOUNTAIN* FAIRY TALE. I HOPE.
OKAY. MAKE THIS ONE COUNT.
BA-BEEP BEEP BOOP

THIS IS *HEALEY!* I'M OUT SAVING THE WORLD RIGHT NOW SO LEAVE A MESSAGE AND I'LL GET RIGHT BACK.
HI HONEY! I KNOW YOU'RE BUSY.
BUT THIS IS REALLY IMPORTANT SO YOU MIGHT WANT TO GET A PEN AND WRITE IT DOWN...

I'VE BEEN DUMPED IN FUCKING MONGROLIA BY YOUR WITCH BITCH ASSISTANT, YOU SELFISH ASSHOLE!
YOU'RE PROBABLY BANGING HER RIGHT NOW!
BOP
HNNT?

I'M Suh-suh-SOOO SORRY....
GRRRRRNNT!
Duh-duh-duh DIDN'T KNOW A-ANYONE WAS Th-th-THERE?
I SAID I WAS SORREEEEEEE!
SHRASH
REEAAAOW!
HELPMEHELP MEHELPME!
SHWUSH
BAROOOONT!
婦女是礦邪魔
Rnnt?
HELP MEEEEEEE!

喝千頭_牛的精液,
山的母親
Roont!
rooont!
rooont!
HELP ME!
HELP ME-- I'M SLIPPING!
WHOEVER YOU ARE-- I C-CAN'T HOLD ON! I...
THE VINES DON'T LOOK LIKE MUCH, BUT THEY WILL HOLD YOUR WEIGHT.
JUST GRAB SOME AND PULL YOURSELF UP.
BATSUKH? SPEAKING ENGLISH?
DON'T THINK. JUST DO IT.
I-- I--I-- I--
YOU GOT IT. YOU GOT IT.
GOOD GIRL.
OHH. OOHHHH. OOOHHHHHH.
OH, BATSUKH...

Batsukh...
Oh, Batsukh...
HAHAHAHA!
Hunh?
WHU? WHERE...?
YOU'RE IN THE YURT. SAFE AND SOUND WITH THE REST OF US.
THANK GOD. I HAD THIS AWFUL NIGHTMARE. IT SEEMED SO...
...REAL.
UH, MAYBE IT WOULD BE A GOOD IDEA TO GIVE THIS COAT TO THE GOODWILL?
AND WITH A REAL MONSTER ON THE LOOSE?
THIS LITTLE YAK NUMBER HAS A LOT GOING FOR IT.

GREEN ZONE ESTATES, SADIST CITY, AFBAGHISTAN
SO SHOULD I WEAR THE CALVIN CLONE WITH THE PLUNGING NECKLINE?
OR THE SEE-THROUGH CHIFFON FROM FRAUDRICK'S OF HOLLYWOOD?
I'M AFRAID I CANNOT VENTUR AN OPINION, MIS POMONA.

I DO NOT UNDERSTAND WHY YOU WISH TO DISPLAY YOUR BREASTS TO SOMEONE WHO IS NOT YOUR HUSBAND OR INFANT CHILD.
BECAUSE SOMETIMES A MEAL TICKET NEEDS PUNCHING.
THE OLD GEEZER MAKES IT POSSIBLE FOR ME TO SELL CARS TO TWERPS LIKE YOU.

BESIDES, I LIKE TO SHOW OFF MY GIRLS.
THEY COST DADDY MORE THAN A COLLEGE EDUCATION.
I AM SURE I AM NOT A GOOD JUDGE OF AMERICAN LIFESTYLES, MS. POMONA.

NO SHIT, SHERLOCK. HOW COME YOU ALWAYS WEAR THE SAME OLD SHIRT AND PANTS?
UHH--I WAS GIVEN INTO YOUR SERVICE ON SUCH SHORT NOTICE THERE WAS NO TIME TO PACK A BAG.
THESE CLOTHES ARE ALL I HAVE. I CAN ASSURE YOU I HAND WASH THEM EACH NIGHT.

AND YOU LOOK LIKE A REFUGEE FROM THE YEAR-END SALE AT A SALVATION ARMY.
I HAVE FRIENDS WHO LEAVE A FEW THINGS HERE. M.C. SCREW'S ABOUT YOUR SIZE.
KIND OF AN URBAN, HIP-HOP THING. TRY IT.
BUT, BUT...

NO BUTS. AND YOU NEEDN'T BE AFRAID OF ME, YOU KNOW.
I'M NOT GOING TO BITE YOU. AT LEAST, NOT TONIGHT...
P-PLEASE, MS. POMONA. ZEROMOSTELIANISM FORBIDS REVEALING ONE'S NAKEDNESS TO THE OPPOSITE SEX BEFORE MARRIAGE.

MY SEMINARY TRAINING IS VERY IMPORTANT TO ME.
THAT'LL CHANGE.
MMM. NOT THE RIGHT ATTITUDE TO PULL OFF A GANGSTA LOOK. I THINK DIEGO'S CRUISING COLORS MIGHT BE MORE YOUR THING.
PERRRRFECT! IF I'M GOING TO HAVE MY OWN PERSONAL HOUSEBOY, THEN THIS IS EXACTLY HOW I WANT HIM TO LOOK.
B-BUT, MS. POMANA-- I CAN'T BE SEEN DRESSED THIS WAY.
NONSENSE! THE FIT IS QUITE FLATTERING. YOU'D BE RIGHT IN TUNE WITH THE ZEITGEIST IF IT WASN'T FOR THE LOOK OF ABJECT TERROR.
WE'LL JUST HAVE TO WORK ON THAT.
I-IT IS NOT POSSIBLE FOR ME, MS. POMONA.
WOULD YOU RATHER I SENT YOU BACK TO YOUR PARENTS, LITTLE HOUSEBOY?
THAT MEANS I'LL BE REPOSSESSING THE ANCESTRAL HOME FOR THE LOAN THEY DEFAULTED ON.
B-BUT...IT IS CONSIDERED A SIN IN MY RELIGION!
I DON'T CARE ABOUT YOUR GODDAMMED HOODOO, ISSA. DIDN'T I MAKE THAT ABUNDANTLY CLEAR?
WHILE YOU'RE WORKING OFF YOUR FAMILY'S DEBT TO ME, I AM GOD.
OUTCH!
BING BONG
BE A DARLING AND ZIP ME UP.
IT'S SHOW TIME.

G-GOOD EVENING.
PLEASE INFORM MS. PEEBLES THAT SECRETARY STELAPHANE HAS ARRIVED.
TELL THE LITTLE FLOWER HER KING BEE IS HERE--AND HE'S BUZZIN'!
MISSSTER SECRETAAARY--I'VE BEEN SOOO LOOKING FORWARD TO OUR LITTLE VISIT!
ISSA--YOU CAN SERVE US IN THE DINING ROOM?
SKIP THE OYSTERS, POMONA. I'VE GOT ENOUGH VIAGRA IN ME TO MAKE RON REAGAN RISE AND SING THE STAR-SPANGLED BANNER.
IF THAT'S THE CASE, I'M SUUUURE YOU REMEMBER WHERE THE DEN OF INIQUITY IS.
I'M SUUURE I DON'T, BUT THEN AGAIN I'M SUUUURE I'LL FIND IT.
EVEN WITH MY NOSE SUPER-GLUED TO YOUR LOVELY CHI-CHIS!
FRICK, DON'T FORGET TO LEAVE MY PHARMACEUTICAL BAG ON THE NIGHT TABLE.
YES SIR.
I WANT TO THANK YOU FOR AUTHORIZING THOSE LAST THREE PLANELOADS OF CARS. WE'VE MADE A KILLING ON THEM.
YOUR OLD MAN IS A HALL OF FAMER IN THE AMERICAN WAY OF LIFE, POMONA.
WARM THE CHOCOLATE BODY PAINT IN THE MICROWAVE.
YES, MA'AM.
YOUR MOOD SEEMS MUCH BRIGHTER THAN THE LAST TIME YOU WERE HERE, MR. SECRETARY.
IT'S THE MOTIVATION & MORALE INITIATIVE I WAS TELLING YOU ABOUT. HEALEY'S PROVED HIMSELF A MARKETING GENIUS.
THE STRATEGIC SITUATION IS TURNING IN OUR FAVOR!

WELL I HOPE THE MILITARY DOESN'T DO ANYTHING DRASTIC--LIKE WINNING THE WAR.
WITH CORPORATE SPONSORSHIP SKYROCKETING, THERE'S LITTLE FEAR OF THAT.
IS THAT TOO HOT? OR NOT ENOUGH?

I HOPE YOU DON'T MIND. THE OYSTERS WERE JUST TOO TEMPTING.
NO, IT IS GOOD THAT THE FOOD NOT GO TO WASTE.
LET ME SERVE YOU.

NO NEED. I'M IN THE SERVICE BUSINESS TOO.
YOU SEEM TO BE HAVING A HARD TIME ADJUSTING TO ITS DEMANDS.
Y-YES. THIS WEEK HAS BEEN THE VERY WORST OF MY LIFE.

IT BEGAN WITH A BOMBING OF THE MARKET OUTSIDE MY HOME.
AND NOW I HAVE BEEN GIVEN OVER TO A CRUEL MISTRESS WHO DEMANDS I TURN MY BACK ON GOD.
AND THIS CREATES CONFLICT IN YOU?

I AM A SIMPLE ZEROMOSTELIAN NOVITIATE, LITTLE SCHOOLED IN THE WAYS OF THE WEST.
TAKE STRENGTH IN THE WORDS OF YOUR PROPHET, THEN...

WASN'T IT BIALYSTOCK WHO TAUGHT THAT GOD ACCOUNTS FOR THE SINS OF A SLAVE ON THE SOUL OF HIS MASTER?
YOU KNOW THE SACRED TEXTS? THEN YOU ARE A SEEKER TOO?

I PRACTICE THE WISE WOMAN WAYS.
YOU MIGHT CALL IT WITCHCRAFT.
I WROTE MY DISSERTATION ON *WICCA!*
THE ROOTS OF ZEROMOSTELIANISM ARE IN THE EARTH RELIGIONS, TOO.
OH, THESE HAVE BEEN SUCH DARK DAYS FOR ME, MAJOR *FRICK.* IT GIVES MY HEART STRENGTH TO MEET SOMEONE WHO SPEAKS THE SAME LANGUAGE OF THE SPIRIT.
I SENSE YOUR QUANDARY IS DEEPER THAN YOU CARE TO ADMIT, *ISSA.*
IT IS TRUE. I...I...AM ONLY JUST A MAN.
I HAVE NEVER BEFORE BEEN FACED WITH SUCH...
TEMPTATION?
I HAVE SOMETHING THAT WILL HELP YOU SATISFY YOUR OBLIGATIONS TO *POMONA* WHILE STAYING IN GOD'S GOOD GRACES.
PLACE IT BETWEEN HER MATTRESS AND HER BOX SPRING.
A CHARM?
THINK OF IT AS A FORM OF DIRECTED PRAYER.
THERE IS AN ABSOLUTE TRUTH CONCERNING THOSE WHO WOULD DOMINATE OTHERS, *ISSA.*
YOUR MISTRESS IS ABOUT TO LEARN IT.

WHAT ARE THEY DOING WITH THOSE ROPES?
TYING OFF THE OLD BULL'S NUTSACK WITH FLANK STRAPS-- JUST LIKE AT THE RODEO.
IT'LL MAKE HIM BUCK AND ACT REAL ORNERY.

ONE PULL OF THE LOOP AND OLD *GENGHIS* WILL GO POSTAL.
HIS HAREM QUEENS WILL FREAK OUT TOO--RIGHT INTO THE CROWD.
THEY'RE GETTING READY TO LEAD THEM INTO THE BIG TOP. C'MON-- LET'S TELL *MORSE.*

SARN'T--THEY'RE MAKING THEIR MOVE. AND IT AIN'T GONNA BE PRETTY.
THEN WE GOTTA SHIT OR GET OFF THE GODDAMMED POT!
PATIENCE, SERGEANT. HERE COMES THE AMBULANCE NOW.

SO WHAT KINDA WEAPON SYSTEM YOU GOT AT YOUR TESTING LAB? CHEMICAL? BIOLOGICAL?
SOMETHIN' MAYBE NOT QUITE READY FOR PRIME TIME?
SINCE YOU SEEM TO HAVE SUCH FAITH IN MY JUDGMENT, SERGEANT, I THINK I'LL LET IT REMAIN A...

...SURPRISE?
HEY, SIS. HOW'S IT GOIN'?

I WAS OVER AT THE HOSPITAL LOOKIN' FOR YA. THEY SAID YOU'D CALLED IN FOR A SPECIAL DELIVERY SO I THOUGHT I'D TAG ALONG.
I'LL DEAL WITH *YOU* IN A MOMENT, BROTHER DEAR.
BEAU, WOULD YOU LIKE TO HELP MUMMY?
OH-KAY.

BE VERY QUIET GOING OVER TO THE ELEPHANT TENT. SLIP THIS INSIDE AND PRESS THE RELEASE BUTTON.
OH-KAY.
HOLD ON JUST A GODDAMN MINUTE. WE CAN'T ENTRUST SOMETHING LIKE THIS TO A FUCKING RETAR--

...*Cough*
UH...*SWITZER. ROYDEN.* TAKE CORPORAL *GEST* TO THE ELEPHANT TENT.
OK, SAR'NT.
HEY, HONEY!
NOT HERE, BABE. I'M WORKING!

YOU GOT *NERVE* SHOWING UP HERE IN AFBAGHISTAN, *LOMAN!*
AFTER YOU BURNED ME ON THE CARTILAGE DEAL, I OUGHTA...
HERE'S WHAT I SKIMMED AND A LITTLE EXTRA. TAKE IT. I WANTCHA' TO HAVE IT.

WHY DO YOU ALWAYS HAVE TO *DO* THIS TO ME? DON'T YOU HAVE A CLUE HOW HARD IT IS WITH *BEAU?*
I KNOW. I KNOW.

"I THINK ABOUT IT ALL THE TIME, SIS. REALLY.
"IT'S JUST... SOMETIMES...
"I CAN'T, LIKE, HELP MYSELF.
"EVER SINCE I WAS A KID, STEALIN' HAS SORT OF BEEN A COMPULSION, Y'KNOW?
"I THINK IT WAS THE OLD MAN.
"I MEAN, SURE I PULLED SOME SHIT ON HIM.
"BUT HE ALWAYS HAD TO OVER-REACT."

BOO FUCKING HOO! YOU THINK I HAD IT EASY GROWING UP UNDER A SOCIOPATH BROTHER?
I'M GONNA GET A THERAPIST THIS TIME. REALLY. REALLY.
BUT THERE'S SOMETHIN' I SORTA NEED YOUR HELP ON.

I WAS WAITING FOR THAT...
NO, IT'S REALLY IMPORTANT. ALLIE'S BEEN KIDNAPPED.
HEALEY'S FINGERPRINTS ARE ALL OVER IT.
YOU WANT TO TALK BUSINESS?

I GOT CASH UP FRONT.

OK.

LET ME WRAP UP ONE *FINAL DETAIL* HERE.

ALL RIGHT, LET'S GET THE MOTHERFUCKING ELEPHANTS OUT FROM UNDER THE CANVAS. HIT 'EM WITH TRANKS IF YOU NEED TO.

SARN'T, *GENGHIS KONG'S* GOT HIS NADS TIED OFF LIKE A BUCKING BRAHMA BULL. NO TRANQUILIZER'S GOING TO KEEP HIM QUIET.

WELL IF YOU'RE SUCH A GODDAMNED EXPERT, *ROYDEN,* WHY DON'T YOU GET IN THERE AND CUT TANTOR'S GRAPES LOOSE.

SERGEANT *MORSE!?* I BELIEVE SOME *GRATITUDE* IS IN ORDER?

OKAY. OKAY. THE MOUSE WAS A NEAT TRICK, MRS. *GEST.* YOU SAVED THE LIVES OF ALL THOSE CIVILIANS AND ANIMALS. AND MAYBE EVEN SOME OF OUR OWN TROOPERS.

I'M NOT ASKING FOR MYSELF! I'M TALKING ABOUT *BEAU!*

HE SHOULD BE T IN FOR A BRONZE STAR *MMEDIATELY.* I'M SURE OLONEL HEALEY WILL BE PPY TO SIGN OFF ON ANY RECOMMENDATION.
WE'LL SEE.
RIGHT NOW I'VE GOT SOMETHIN' THAT I PROMISED *BEAU* A LONG TIME AGO.

HERE YA GO, CORPORAL.
I BETTER NOT SEE YA YAKKIN' INTO IT IN COMBAT.
A PHONE?!
IT'S ABOUT *TIME* MY SON WAS TREATED WITH THE SAME RESPECT AS THE OTHER SOLDIERS. I HOPE IT'S THE LATEST MODEL WITH ALL THE FEATURES?

IT'S A STANDARD ISSUE CELL PHONE FRESH OUT OF THE BOX. CODED NUMBER WITH QUANTUM ENCRYPTION.
IT SHOULD HAVE A DECENT RING TONE.
I TOOK THE LIBERTY OF SELECTING THE NUMBER ONE ON THE HIT PARADE.

BUT HOW COME NOBODY'S CALLING ME?
I WILL CALL YOU, MY BEAUTIFUL BOY!
WE'LL TALK EVERY DAY ABOUT HOW SERGEANT *MORSE* IS RESPONDING TO YOUR SPECIAL NEEDS.
I JUST ACTIVATED YOUR MILITARY *ID*, SO IT WILL BE A WHILE BEFORE ANYONE...

WE'LL BE SETTIN' OUT FOR HEAVEN IN MY LITTLE SPEED BOAT!
HEY! IT'S RINGING! IT'S RINGING! SOMEONE'S CALLING ME UP!
HOW EXCITING! YOUR VERY FIRST PHONE CALL! LET ME GET A SHOT!

HULLO?
HI! DID YOU KNOW THAT YOU MIGHT BE PAYING TOO MUCH FOR LONG DISTANCE SERVICES? PRESS 1 TO START SAVING MONEY IMMEDIATELY!
I WAS JUST GETTING READY TO SNIP THE ROPE WHEN HE BUCKED AND...
Snzzz

MOTIVATION
HOT ZONE
MORALE

MOKTA, AFBAGHISTAN.
OOOH. IS THIS MAN DRUNK, MICHI?
HE'S DEAD.
DON'T YOU KNOW ANYTHING?

A FEW YEARS FROM NOW.
DID HE HAVE A HEART ATTACK?
HARDLY. HE'S BEEN DRILLED WITH POWER TOOLS.

HE USED TO RUN THE MOTEL SIXTY. NOW HE'S A ONE NIGHT STAND FOR THE FLIES.
WHY DO FLIES LIKE HIM?

BECAUSE THEY MAKE BABY FLIES INSIDE HIM, STUPID

DON'T YOU KNOW ANYTHING?

LET'S GO SEE IF MAI MAU'S VISITORS HAVE LEFT YET.
YOU MEAN THE CHINAMEN?
BONTCH

THEY'RE NORTH KOREENIANS. AND KEEP YOUR MOUTH SHUT ABOUT IT.
OR THE FLIES WILL BE MAKING BABIES IN YOU.

FIFTY-EIGHT. FIFTY-NINE. SIXTY THOUSAND. EVERYTHING'S IN ORDER, COLONEL DONG.
MY COMPLIMENTS ON THE QUALITY OF YOUR BILLS, TOO.
I HOPE THE AMERICAN'S CELL PHONE IS PROVING TO BE A BENEFICIAL ACQUISITION?
VERY MUCH SO. YES.
POPULAR MECHANICALS REPORTS THEIR QUANTUM ENCRYPTION CAN'T BE BROKEN WITHOUT SPLITTING THE FLOW OF SPACE-TIME.
HAVE YOU SUCCEEDED?
A FLY IN THE HOUSE OF LOVE
NOTHING SO DRAMATIC. WE'RE HOPING TO HARVEST FRESHLY GENERATED MILITARY PHONE NUMBERS BEFORE THEY ARE ASSIGNED.
IF WE ARE SO FORTUNATE, THEN WE'LL SLIP IN A BIT OF OUR CODE BEFORE THE DATA IS PLACED IN A POCKET DIMENSION.
ONCE WE'VE GOT A LINK, LIEUTENANT BOA HERE WILL WORK TO SUBVERT THE WILL OF ITS OWNER.
WHO LET ALL THESE DAMN FLIES IN HERE? MICHI?

IT'S NOT Y FAULT!
FZZZZZZ
THE MOTEL CLERK'S OUT FRONT AND HE'S COVERED WITH THEM.
WE'D BETTER LEAVE BEFORE THE AUTHORITIES ARRIVE. THANK YOU FOR YOUR ASSISTANCE.
THANK YOU, COLONEL DONG.

NEEDLESS TO SAY, IF YOU TURN UP ANYTHING MORE, PLEASE THINK OF US FIRST.
BONTCH
WE WILL. AND DON'T BE STRANGERS!

ANYTHING GOOD ON?
I NEED TO WATCH THE PACO LIPSYNC SPECIAL!
ANOTHER ONE?
YES, THEY'RE GOING TO HAVE A SEANCE AND TALK TO THE BAND ON THE OTHER SIDE!
MONKEY CHASING WEASEL
BINGO.
I'M FINALLY GETTING SOMETHING ON THIS FLY ON THE WALL PIECE OF SHIT.
ACTUALLY IT'S KIND OF COOL.
GOT SOME REALLY NEAT BELLS AND WHISTLES. LIKE A HORMONE SCENT THAT ATTRACTS OR REPELS REAL FLIES, DEPENDING ON THE SITUATION.
THAT FEATURE'S STILL IN BETA THOUGH.
WHAT WILL THEY THINK OF NEXT?

EXACTLY MY RESPONSE WHEN I'M EAVESDROPPING ON SOME OF THE THINGS PEOPLE DO.
BUT FROM WHAT I'M SEEING HERE, IT LOOKS LIKE SITUATION-NORMAL OVER AT JENAN'S PAD.
GOOD. GOOD. ANY OTHER STORM CLOUDS ON THE HORIZON?
NOT SINCE YOU LET THE ALLIE AND STELAPHANE PROBLEMS SOLVE THEMSELVES.
REAL LEADERSHIP THERE, SIR. HOW DO YOU WANT THE BACK?
IT WAS THE RIGHT CALL AT THE RIGHT TIME.
BRING OUT THAT WAVE OVER MY EARS.
THE HOT ZONE CLUB CAMPAIGN IS PUTTING UP SOME PRETTY SERIOUS NUMBERS.
BIG FINGER'S CHARTING DEEP PENETRATION OF TARGET DEMOGRAPHICS UP AND DOWN THE SPECTRUM. WE GOT A SIX PERCENT BUMP IN RECRUITING IN JUST THE FIRST WEEK.
LISTEN AND LEARN, YOUNG'UNS! DIDN'T I SEE IT, FIRST? DIDN'T I?
IT TAKES CREATIVE VISION TO WEAVE THOSE GOLDEN THREADS INTO THE CONSUMER'S MEDIA COCOON.
A BEANCOUNTER LIKE STELAPHANE CAN'T DO IT BECAUSE HE'S GOT NO SOUL.
SHOULDN'T WE BE ENGAGING IN SOME SERIOUS FORWARD THINKING ON THIS, SIR?
MONKEY CHASING WEASEL
I MEAN, IF THIS HOT ZONE THING IS REALLY MORE THAN THE USUAL DOG AND PONY SHOW...
...THEN YOU'RE GOING TO WANT TO OWN IT, RIGHT?

FORWARD OPERATING BASE HABITRAIL
BABEL PROVINCE, AFBAGHISTAN.
FLABB-DUDE, YOU LOSER! LOOK WHAT I GOT AT THE CIRCUS!
IT'S A MAGIC MONKEY. TELLS FORTUNES AND SHIT.
HEY, ROYDEN. WAS SWITZER OVER THERE?
YEAH! YEAH! IT WAS INSANE. I SHIT YOU NOT-- WE HAD THE HADJ GETTING TRAMPLED BY ELEPHANTS, MAN.
SHOULDA BEEN THERE. IT WAS ONE FOR THE AGES.
YEAH, WELL, MORSE'S STILL GOT ME SCRATCHED OFF COMBAT OPERATIONS.
I DON'T MIND DOING TRASH PICK-UP. SWITZER'S SQUAT IS ON THIS RUN...
FLABB-DUDE-- I AM DETERMINED TO GET YOU OFF THIS SAPPY EMO SHIT.
IN FACT, THAT'S WHY I SCORED THE MAGIC MONKEY. SEE, HE CAME WITH THIS BOOK...
MAGIC
SHHH! IT'S SWITZER! AND SHE'S GOT SOMEONE WITH HER.
ANY LUCK FINDING OUT WHAT HAPPENED TO ALLIE?
DEE DEE'S LOOKING INTO IT.
SHE'S GOT ALL KINDS OF CONTACTS OVER HERE. Y'KNOW-- FROM WORKIN' AT THE HOSPITAL.
BUT SHE'S GOT SO MUCH ON HER PLATE WITH BEAU AND EVERYTHING.
HEY, WE'RE FAMILY. WE TAKE CARE OF EACH OTHER, Y'KNOW?
WHO'S THAT GOIN' INSIDE WITH HER?
DUDE SHOWED UP DURING THE ELEPHANT DANCE. I THINK IT'S HER HUSBAND.
HERE? IN THE BAGH?
WHAT'S UP WITH THAT?

SPEAKING ABOUT TAKING CARE OF FAMILY...
I SMELL LIKE A ZOO.
POUR ME A CHARDONNAY WHILE I HOP IN THE SHOWER AND SCRAPE DOWN.
I'LL BRING THE BOTTLE AND JOIN YOU.
NOW *THAT* IS BEING A GOOD HUBBY!
SHE'S GONNA DO HIM. RIGHT HERE! NOW!
I CAN'T BELIEVE IT!
DUDE, THEY'RE ***MARRIED.*** NOW COME ON. DON'T ***EMBARRASS*** YOURSELF IN FRONT OF MY MAGIC MONKEY, OKAY?

HE'S GOT THIS ***BOOK***, SEE?
THE GUY WHO SOLD HIM TO ME SAID THE LITTLE GOOBER COULD HELP WITH THAT ***MOJO*** THE WICCAN SLAPPED ON YA!
I'VE BEEN TRYING TO TELL YOU, ***ROYDEN...***

THIS DOESN'T HAVE A THING TO DO WITH ***FRICK*** OR HER LOVE CHARMS.
AND EVEN IF IT DID-- IT WOULDN'T MATTER.
WHAT DO YOU ***SAY***, MAGIC MONKEY? CAN THIS ONCE-PROUD PATHETIC LOSER BE SAVED?

HAHAHA!
OOOOH YEEAAHHH.
Eeep Eep.
BREAKING SPELLS

MMMM. YOU GOT E MAGIC INGERS.
WHAT AM I GONNA DO, **ROYDEN?** I--I CAN'T LET THEM JUST...
RELAX. AND LET YOUR FINGERS DIAL UP A CASE OF COITUS INTERRUPTUS.
WE'LL BE SETTIN' OUT FOR HEAVEN IN OUR LITTLE SPEED BOAT...
DON'T.
IT MIGHT BE IMPORTANT.
BUSY! WHO **ELSE** WOULD BE...?
DADDY! HI! IT'S SO **GREAT** TO HEAR YOUR VOICE!
HOW'S MOM?

OH, HEY, REVEREND. YEAH, I WAS MISSING MY LITTLE SWEET PATOOTIE, SO I FLEW OVER FOR A COUPLE DAYS.
WE'RE JUST KICKIN' BACK AND, Y'KNOW, RELAXING.
I'VE GOT A MESSAGE FROM PEEBLES. HE CLEANED UP EVERYTHING WITH THE COPS.
AND HE'S WORKING ON THE DAMAGE TO THE HOUSE.
BUT I HAVE TO WARN YOU; WHEN NEEDHAWK AND BLANCHE GET OUT OF THE BURN UNIT, THEY'RE GOING TO BE KNOCKING ON YOUR DOOR.
...and then we sew him back up, see?
LISTEN, LOMAN, I'M PREPARED TO FORGIVE THE INCIDENT WITH THE CHURCH SLUSH FUND.
BUT I DON'T WANT MY LITTLE GIRL GETTING INVOLVED IN ANY OF THIS.
SHE'S AN INNOCENT.
OF COURSE SHE IS, SIR.
YES, I UNDERSTAND.
IT'S WHAT WE ALL LOVE ABOUT HER.
FLABB-DUDE, MY FRIEND, THE MAGIC MONKEY AND I HAVE DECIDED YOU ARE A DANGER TO YOURSELF.
IT'S TIME TO PLAY SOME SERIOUS WITCHDOCTOR.

GREEN ZONE ESTATES
SADIST CITY, AFBAGHISTAN
OH, BABY, IT WAS JUST SOOOO FABULOUS HAVING YOU OVER FOR PLAYTIME.
AND YOU'RE JUST SUCH A STALLION SINCE YOU GOT YOUR LITTLE BLUE PILLS.
UH HUH.

SO, UH... MAYBE WE COULD MEET FOR LUNCH SOMETIME?
MM HMM.
I'D LOVE TO DISCUSS GETTING A FEW MORE PLANELOADS OF CARS INTO THE COUNTRY.

WE'VE HAD SOME PROBLEMS ON THE SUPPLY END, BUT DADDY SAYS INVENTORY IS FULL AGAIN.
I GOT MEETINGS.
TOMORROW I'M FREE. WE COULD...
REMEMBER-- THE CHARM MUST BE USED WISELY. AND WITH COMPASSION.

mumble mumble

CALL ME?

OR I'LL CALL YOU?

OKAY...?

WHAT THE FUCK ARE YOU MUMBLING ABOUT?

I--I'M JUST...

...PRAYING.

BZZZZT! WRONG ANSWER! YOU DON'T PRAY IN THIS HOUSE!

I'M THE MISTRESS AROUND HERE, WHICH MEANS I OWN YOUR GOD-FEARING ASS, LOCK, STOCK AND CLENCHED CHEEKS!

NOW GET ME A BLOODY MARY AND A SLICED CUCUMBER.

AND DRAW ME A BATH.

LISTEN--IT ISN'T JUST **YOU.** IT'S **ALL** THAT SANCTIMONIOUS RELIGIOUS CRAP THAT BURNS MY ASS.

YOU PEOPLE ARE **ALWAYS** CRITICIZING ANYONE WHO'S COMFORTABLE WITH THEIR OWN SEXUALITY.

IF YOU'LL PARDON, MA'AM. IT IS NOT ONE'S APPROACH TO HONEST SEXUAL RELATIONS THAT COMES INTO QUESTION...

IT IS HOW ONE MIGHT INCORPORATE THEIR SEXUALITY WITH **COMMERCE** THAT WE SEE AS MORALLY PROBLEMATIC.

WHICH IS PRECISELY WHY I'M THE MISTRESS AND **YOU'RE** THE SLAVE.

YOU DON'T HAVE A **CLUE** WHAT IT TAKES TO MAKE IT BIG IN TODAY'S WORLD.

OR WHAT AN ABSOLUTE **ACHIEVEMENT** IT IS FOR A WOMAN TO BE THE MISTRESS OF A **TRULY** POWERFUL MAN.

haha

ARE YOU LAUGHIN' AT ME, YOU RUBE PIECE OF SHIT?

NO, MA'AM. I JUST FIND IT AMUSING HOW THE SAME WORD CAN HAVE **OPPOSITE** MEANINGS.

YOU ARE **MY** MISTRESS AND THAT MEANS I MUST SERVE YOU.

BUT WHEN YOU ARE **HIS** MISTRESS, IT IS **YOU** WHO ARE IN BONDAGE.

FUCK YOU!
SMASH
IF THIS WAS FIVE HUNDRED YEARS AGO, I'D HAVE YOUR TONGUE CUT OUT!

GET ME A FRESH DRINK. AND MY PHONE, DAMMIT.
I'VE GOT TO SCHEDULE A TUNEUP.

Babylon General Hospital
DEE DEE GEST.
HI, DEE DEE--IT'S POMONA.
GIRLFRIEND! I WAS JUST REACHING FOR THE PHONE TO CALL YOU!

SO HOW'S THE LOVE LIFE? STILL PUTTING UP WITH THAT BAD BOY, STELAPHANE?
FRANKLY, DEE DEE, I'M A LITTLE WORRIED. LAST NIGHT HE DIDN'T SEEM QUITE AS ENTHRALLED WITH MY CHI-CHIS AS HE HAS BEEN ON PREVIOUS OCCASIONS.

TIME TO TRICK OUT THE CHASSIS? NOT TO WORRY, I'LL SET YOU UP WITH THE GUY WHO DOES MADONNA AND LOURDES.
BUT WHAT'S THIS I HEAR ABOUT STELAPHANE FLYING ALLIE HEALEY INTO THE BAGH?
OOOH, NOW THERE'S A STORY FOR YOU!

LAST NIGHT THE OLD COOT GOT INTO THE MARCHING POWDER AND COULDN'T SHUT UP ABOUT HER.
APPARENTLY, ALLIE FOUND OUT HEALEY'S BEEN TAPPING ONE OF THE LOCALS AND TRIES TO KILL HERSELF.
STELAPHANE STOPS HER AND BRINGS HER OVER HERE IN A STRAIGHTJACKET. THEN HEALEY FLIPS OUT.

SUPPOSEDLY HEALEY'S SECRETARY HAD TO TAKE OVER AND SHE AND STELAPHANE CUT SOME SORT OF DEAL FOR SPONSORSHIP OR SOMETHING.
THEY END UP AGREEING, FOR HEALEY'S SANITY, THAT ALLIE HAS TO GO.
THEY *Crunch crunch* SANCTIONED HER?

NO. THEY'VE GOT PLACES WHERE THEY PERMANENTLY DISAPPEAR PEOPLE.
AND, FRANKLY, WHEN IT COMES TO MRS. MANIC-DEPRESSIVE, HEALEY SHOULD HAVE HAD IT DONE YEARS AGO.

WINTER PASTURE, SINKYANG FRONTIER OUTER MONGROLIAN REPUBLIC
I'M CRAZY...
I DON'T KNOW WHY I'M DOING THIS...
I WAS SO STUPID TO AGREE TO IT...
THE OTHER WIVES DON'T THINK YOU'RE STUPID, ALLIE.
THEY SUSPECT YOU HAVE BEWITCHED BATSUKH.
HE WASN'T THIS EAGER WHEN HE BROUGHT EACH OF US TO THE MARRIAGE BOWER.
EVER SINCE HE SAVED ME FROM THAT CREATURE, HE'S BEEN LOOKING AT ME WITH THE STRANGEST EXPRESSION.
BATSUKH KNOWS THE MOTHER OF MOUNTAIN ONLY SHOWS HERSELF TO VERY SPECIAL WOMEN.
我們使沉醉修飾到達
OH, MY GOD. HE'S HERE. NOW WHAT?
NOW YOU WILL BE MARRIED!
BUT IS IT A GOOD CAREER MOVE? I...
BETROTHED, I HAVE PREPARED OUR BOWER AND WEDDING FEAST.
ACCEPT THESE REINS AS THE HARNESS OF MY HEART.
BUT I'M ALREADY...
I MEAN, I KNOW YOU'RE ALREADY...
I'M NOT SURE IF BIGAMY IS SOMETHING I WANT TO EXPERIMENT WITH RIGHT NOW.

YOU RIDE WELL.
THANKS. GROWING UP IN NEW JERSEY, EVERY GIRL HAS TO HAVE A HORSE.
SO CAN WE TALK NOW?
YOU SPEAK ENGLISH PRETTY WELL. AT LEAST WHEN YOU WANT TO.
AND YOU SOUND SO... FAMILIAR. IT'S KIND OF WEIRD.
I USED TO LIVE IN L.A. DID VOICE-OVERS FOR ADVERTISING SPOTS.
OH MY GOD--YES! YOU'RE THE POLKA COLA GUY! "POLK ME, POLK YOU!"
YOU'RE REALLY FAMOUS!
ONLY TO THOSE POOR SOULS WHO PLACE SPIRITUAL VALUE ON CHEMICALLY FLAVORED SUGAR WATER.
I LEFT THAT ILLUSION BEHIND LONG AGO.
MY REAL LIFE BEGAN WHEN I RETURNED TO THE STEPPES OF MY ANCESTORS.
HERE I FOUND GOD'S PURPOSE FOR ME.
IT IS THE GREATEST TREASURE.
YEAH, BUT THEY DON'T EVEN HAVE, LIKE... THE INTERNET OUT HERE.
I THANK GOD IN EVERY WAKING AND SLEEPING MOMENT THAT I AM FOREVER FREE OF SUCH DEVICES.
THEY ONLY SERVE AS A REMINDER THAT THE MACHINE WORLD RUNS ON ENNUI.
COME, ALLIE. CELEBRATE WHAT IS REAL WITH ME.
OUR BOWER AWAITS.

YOU DID ALL THIS FOR... ME?
THE CATERING MUST HAVE COST YOU A FORTUNE!
YOUR SOUL IS A THRONE UPON WHICH SITS THE KING OF CREATION. COULD YOU DESERVE ANY LESS?
I DON'T GET ALL THE NEW AGEY STUFF, BUT I MUST ADMIT... I KIND OF LIKE THIS.
AND I'M THINKING TO HELL WITH THE JERKY HUSBAND WHO NEVER RETURNS MY CALLS.
REGRETS ARE LEAVES DANCING ON THE AUTUMN WIND.
I HAVE PREPARED OUR RITUAL WEDDING MEAL WITH MY OWN HANDS.
AS WE PARTAKE OF THIS, LET US PARTAKE OF EACH OTHER.
OOOKAY. WHY NOT?
NEVER KNOW. MAYBE I CAN WRITE A BESTSELLER SOMEDAY.
MMM! THIS IS GOOD, I CAN'T STOP EATING IT.
YOU COOKED IT YOURSELF? WHAT'S IN IT?
THE PRESCRIBED INGREDIENTS ARE GOOSE FAT, YAK BLUBBER AND BOAR SUET.
IT IS CONSIDERED THE GREATEST GIFT A GROOM CAN BESTOW UPON HIS BRIDE.
TRADITION SAYS WE MUST STAY IN OUR BOWER UNTIL THE WHOLE POT IS CONSUMED.
YOU KNOW WHAT? I HAVE TO, UH...GO USE THE LITTLE GIRLS' ROOM?
OF COURSE I HAVE PREPARE A FRES PIT DOW IN THE RAVINE.

I'M SUCH A FUCKING PIG!
PIG! PIG! PIG! PIG! PIIIG!

PIGGYPIGGY PICHUUUUUUUUP!
Wraautch!

YOU... YOU...REFUSE OUR WEDDING FEAST?
IT'S NOT THAT. Kof I JUST CAN'T LET MYSELF EAT ALL THIS FOOD...
IT'S TOO FATTY...
AND I'M ON A STRICT DIET...

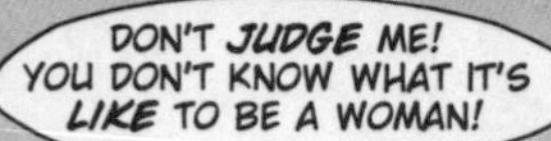
DON'T JUDGE ME! YOU DON'T KNOW WHAT IT'S LIKE TO BE A WOMAN!
THERE'S ALL THESE EXPECTATIONS ABOUT WEIGHT. THE WAY EVERYONE LOOKS AT YOU.
ALL THOSE FASHION MAGAZINES.

I STAND NOT IN JUDGMENT, ALLIE...

BUT TAKE MY LEAVE IN MOURNING.

BATSUKH?

SO I CAN BE A LITTLE Chomp OBSESSIVE-COMPULSIVE SOMETIMES.
IT'S PROBABLY A GOOD THING WE GOT IT OUT IN THE OPEN chomf RIGHT AT THE START.

YOU'RE SO GENTLE AND FORGIVING.
I THOUGHT MONGROLIANS WERE ALL BLOODTHIRSTY BARBARIANS RAMPAGING ACROSS THE STEPPES.
THE EXACT *OPPOSITE* IS TRUE. WE CONQUERED MANY LANDS, YES...
BUT WE WERE WARRIORS OF *LOVE.*

THEN AND NOW, WE BELIEVE OUR GOD-GIVEN DUTY IS TO CHANGE THE WORLD FOR THE BETTERMENT OF ALL.
WE EFFECT *CHANGE* IN THOSE WHO HAVE BEEN SICKENED AND WOUNDED BY THE EMOTIONAL PLAGUE THAT AFFLICTS MANKIND.
SO I'M LIKE SOME SORT OF *REFUGEE* TO YOU?

YOU'RE *MUCH* MORE THAN THAT, *ALLIE.* I KNEW IT WHEN THE *MOTHER OF MOUNTAIN* SHOWED HERSELF TO YOU.
NONE OF MY OTHER WIVES HAVE BEEN SO BLESSED BY THE *MOTHER.*

LET ME GUIDE YOU INTO THAT MOST SACRED JUNCTURE WHERE HEART AND SENSES MEET.
BY FALLING DEEPLY... TRULY... TOTALLY...
...IN LOVE.
Ohhhh...

OOOOOOO

ROUND AND ROUND THE MULBERRY BUSH, THE MONKEY CHASED THE WEASEL...
IT'S PACO LIPSYNC! FROM BEYOND THE GRAVE!
SHH! THEY'RE GOING TO PLAY THEIR NEW REMIX OF "LITTLE SPEEDBOAT"!

THIS IS CRAZY.
YOU THINK THAT'S CRAZY-- LISTEN TO THIS: POPULAR MECHANICALS SAYS THE U.S. MILITARY WILL BE UTILIZING TIME TRAVEL BY 2015.

WELL, IF THEY'RE TALKING ABOUT IT, YOU KNOW THEY'VE ALREADY GOT IT.
SEE, THAT'S JUST WHAT THEY WANT YOU TO THINK.

WHRRRRR

IF THERE'S TIME TRAVELERS FROM THE FUTURE, WE'D HAVE MET THEM BY NOW. THEY'D BE TRYING TO SELL US SOMETHING.

WE'RE SORRY! THE FLY ON THE WALL ADVANCED INSECT SURVEILLANCE DRONE IS EXPERIENCING MOMENTARY COMMUNICATIONS DIFFICULTY. ☹
AHH, BALLS!

BING BONG
OH DEAR. SOMEONE'S AT THE DOOR. GET IT, MICHI.
I HAVE TO HEAR THIS!
I'LL DO IT.

COLONEL DONG AND LIEUTENANT BOA! WHAT A SURPRISE!
SINCERE APOLOGIES IF WE BARGE IN AT A BAD TIME.
FOR HEAVEN'S SAKE, NO! YOU'RE FAMILY, COLONEL!
GOOD! GOOD! WE HAVE AN INTERESTING NEW PROPOSAL THAT WE HOPE YOU WILL CONSIDER.
FIRST, LET US SHARE THE GOOD NEWS. WE HAVE SUCCEEDED IN EXTRACTING THE UNENCRYPTED NUMBER OF ONE RECRUIT FROM THE CELL PHONE YOU SOLD US.
SPLTCH
FZZZZZ
CERTAINLY THAT CAN'T BE ENOUGH?
IN THIS GAME, IT'S PLENTY. LIEUTENANT BOA WILL SOON BE TARGETING THE SOLDIER WITH DEEP-PSYCHE OPERATIONS.
WHAT'S YOUR STRATEGY? MANCHURIAN CANDIDATE? TURN HIM INTO A LEE HARVEY OSWALD?
NOTHING SO SENSATIONAL. OUR RADIANT LEADER TELLS US WE ARE NOT CURRENTLY AT WAR WITH THE UNITED STATES.
ONLY IN COMPETITION.
THE FLY ON THE WALL ADVANCED INSECT SURVEILLANCE DRONE IS STILL EXPERIENCING MOMENTARY COMMUNICATIONS DIFFICULTY.
PLEASE STAND BY. YOUR BUSINESS IS IMPORTANT TO US.
FUCK YOU, SNOT BAG!

WE WOULD LIKE TO SUGGEST EXPANDING OUR WORKING RELATIONSHIP FOR OUR MUTUAL BENEFIT.
WHAT'S YOUR PITCH, DONG?
WE'RE VERY INTERESTED IN THIS COLONEL HEALEY FELLOW. HIS STAR SEEMS TO BE ON THE RISE IN THE AMERICAN MILITARY ESTABLISHMENT.
FZZZZZZ
WE SEEK AN ARRANGEMENT BY WHICH WE REWARD YOU FOR, PERHAPS, REKINDLING YOUR FRIENDSHIP WITH THE COLONEL.
FZZZZZZ
WHAT DO YOU WANT? THAT I MARRY THAT CONCEITED BLOWHARD?
YOU COULDN'T PRINT ENOUGH CURRENCY TO BUY THAT.
FZZZZZZ
WE MEAN NOTHING OF THE SORT, MADAM. AND I HOPE NO OFFENSE IS TAKEN.
HE LIKES TO TALK. YOU LIKE TO LISTEN. THAT'S AS FAR AS IT NEED GO.
FZZZZZ
POONT
Polka Cola
FZZZZZZ
WE'LL PAY YOU HANDSOMELY FOR ANY USEFUL INSIDE INFORMATION YOU MIGHT BE ABLE TO GLEAN FROM YOUR CONVERSATIONS.
FZZZZ
NOW WHAT THE HELL IS GOING ON?
Polka Cola

EWWW! DISGUSTING!
MICHI I TOLD YOU NOT TO LEAVE YOUR EMPTY POP BOTTLES AROUND!
SHH! SHH! THEY'RE JUST GOING TO CHOOSE REPLACEMENT BAND MEMBERS!

GET THESE FLIES OUT OF HERE THIS INSTANT OR I'LL REPLACE YOU! PERMANENTLY!
OH GROSS!
THEY'RE MATING!

I DON'T SEE ANY BABY FLIES, MICHI.
THEY'RE THE MAGGOTS! DON'T YOU KNOW ANYTHING?
WATCH ME SHAKE THESE TWO LOVERS UP.

NOW LET THEM TRY AND DO THEIR DIRTY BUSINESS!

SO MICHI, THOSE TWO ON THE MAN'S TONGUE...?

THAT'S HOW OUR MOMMIES AND DADDIES DO IT?

FOOOMF
OF COURSE IT IS!

DON'T YOU KNOW ANYTHING?

THANK YOU... FOR CHOOSING...
THE FLY ON... THE WALL ANCED... INSECTILE SURVEILLANCE DRONE...
BROUGHT TO YOU... BY RADIO-8...
KILLS BUGS... RIGHT WHERE THEY...
SWAT
Thank... you...
for... choosing...
the fly on the wall... advanced... insectile... surveillance... drone... drone... drone... drone...
YOU ASTOUND ME, MAI MAU!
WE'RE SORRY! THIS FLY ON THE WALL INSECTILE SURVEILLANCE DRONE HAS SUFFERED A SYSTEMS FAILURE OF UNKNOWN ORIGIN. A REPORT HAS BEEN ISSUED TO BIG FINGER.
THANK YOU FOR CHOOSING RADIO-8! KILLS BUGS RIGHT WHERE THEY LIVE!
FUCKING COCK VOMIT!

KNOCK KNOCK. IT'S ME--DEE DEE. YOU ALONE?
YEAH. WOYNER AND HEALEY DECIDED THEY FORGOT SOMETHING BACK AT THE HOTEL.
WE HAVEN'T HAD TIME TO DISCUSS BEAU'S MEDAL YET, THOUGH.

ACTUALLY I'M HERE ON OTHER BUSINESS.
SAFE TO TALK?
LET'S WALK ON THE BEACH. WHITE NOISE FROM THE WAVES WILL COVER US.
YOU MENTIONED A CERTAIN PHARMACEUTICAL PRODUCT TO ME THE LAST TIME I WAS IN.
A CREATIVITY DRUG?

YEAH! EXTADRINE! IT MAPS ALL THE CREATIVE CIRCUITS IN THE USER'S BRAIN TO BIG FINGER'S COLLECTIVE UNCONSCIOUS.
PACO LIPSYNC'S ROAD MANAGER TOLD ME THAT'S WHAT THE BAND USED TO WRITE "LITTLE SPEEDBOAT."
FOR OBVIOUS REASONS, ITS NOT SOMETHING THEY'RE EVER GOING TO RELEASE ON THE MARKET.

BUT THE GUY RUNNING THE HOSPITAL MORGUE IS A FRIEND OF MINE. HE FOUND THESE ON ONE OF THE BAND MEMBERS WHEN THEY BROUGHT THEM IN.
TAAAASTY! THERE'S ENOUGH THERE TO WRITE AN ALBUM!
WHAT'S THE DAMAGE?
EXTADRINE
NO CASH OUTLAY REQUIRED. JUST INFORMATION.
I NEED REAL-TIME COORDINATES.
ON ALLIE HEALEY.

28 IF
VEITCH
ERSKINE

SINKYANG FRONTIER,
OUTER MONGROLIAN REPUBLIC
A FEW YEARS FROM NOW.
I SHOULD HAVE KNOWN.
YOU'D BE LONG...
...GONE.
BATSUKH?

IT'S A BEAUTIFUL MORNING FOR A RIDE, ***ALLIE!***

WILL YOU JOIN MONGOL AND ME IN THE HIGH CHAPARRAL?

SURE, BUT... IS THERE, LIKE, A ***FIRE EXTINGUISHER*** AROUND HERE?

FOOLS RUSH IN

I WAS TRYING TO HEAT UP THE STEW FOR BREAKFAST.
BUT ALL MY FIRE MADE WAS SMOKE.
I'M PLEASED OUR WEDDING FEAST IS BEGINNING TO AGREE WITH YOU.

FOR A QUICK HOT FIRE YOU TAKE THE DRIEST TWIGS AND BREAK THEM UP INTO SMALL PIECES. SEE?
YOU KNOW, I ACTUALLY LEARNED THIS BACK IN GIRLS SCOUTS. NEVER THOUGHT I'D HAVE TO USE IT...

WHEN I WAS DOING VOICEOVERS BACK IN L.A., I HAD A BUMPER STICKER THAT SAID "HORSE WHISPERERS DO IT BY TOUCH."

I HOPE I'VE TOUCHED SOMETHING IN YOU.

DO WE **HAVE** TO GO RIDING IN THE HIGH CHAPARRAL?

THIS IS OUR **BOWER** TIME, **ALLIE.** AT LEAST UNTIL THE RITUAL STEW IS COMPLETELY CONSUMED.

WE CAN DO WHATEVER WE WISH.

IS THIS WHY YOU GET MARRIED SO OFTEN?

SINCE I RETURNED TO MY HOMELAND, I'VE LEARNED TO RECOGNIZE GOD'S FACE IN **ALL** WOMEN.

BUT THERE'S A VERY SPECIAL RADIANCE I SEE IN YOU, **ALLIE.**

MOTHER OF MOUNTAIN SENSED IT TOO.

THE MACHINE WORLD FORCES ALL WHO INHABIT IT TO DENY THE LIGHT WITHIN.

I WANT YOU TO SEE YOUR RADIANCE, **ALLIE.** REFLECTED THROUGH ME.

FORWARD OPERATING BASE HABITRAIL
BABEL PROVINCE, AFBAGHISTAN
TIRED OF BEING LORD OF THE FLIES YET, FLABB-DUDE?
I'M SICK OF SPENDING EVERY WAKING MOMENT THINKING ABOUT SWITZER. THAT'S FOR SURE.

THEN IT'S TIME TO PUT MY MAGIC MONKEY TO WORK FOR YOU.
THIS BOOK SAYS HE CAN BREAK ANY KIND OF SPELL. YOU JUST GOTTA WANT TO DO IT.
I'LL TRY ANYTHING AT THIS POINT.
MAGIC

OKEY-DOKE. SAYS HERE THAT EACH SPELL AFFECTS A CERTAIN PART OF THE ASTRAL BODY.
SO WE LET THE MAGIC MONKEY PAW ALL AROUND YOU UNTIL IT FINDS WHERE THIS LOVE THING IS HIDIN' OUT.
RIGHT.

SEE! YOU BEEN THINKIN' ABOUT HER OBSESSIVELY. SO MAGIC MONKEY'S WRAPPIN' HIMSELF ALL AROUND YOUR HEAD.
NEXT YOU START CHANTING "LOVE BEGONE!" GIVE IT ALL YOU GOT.
OKAY. BUT WHAT'S HE DOING BACK THERE?

WHAT'S WITH THE FASHION SHOW, FLABBERGAST? YOU'RE SUPPOSED TO BE SLOPPIN' OUT THE FUCKING SHITTER!
LOVE BEGONE! LOVE BEGONE! LOVE BEGONE!
FLAB-DUDE'S GETTIN' HIS MOJO BACK, SAR'NT. I'LL ROCK THE MOP FOR HIM.

I FUCKING SWEAR. JUST WHEN YOU THINK THIS COCKAMAMIE WAR COULDN'T GET ANY MORE FUCKING BUGSHIT...
HERE COMES THE MOMOMOBILE!
GRUNNNGRUUNNN

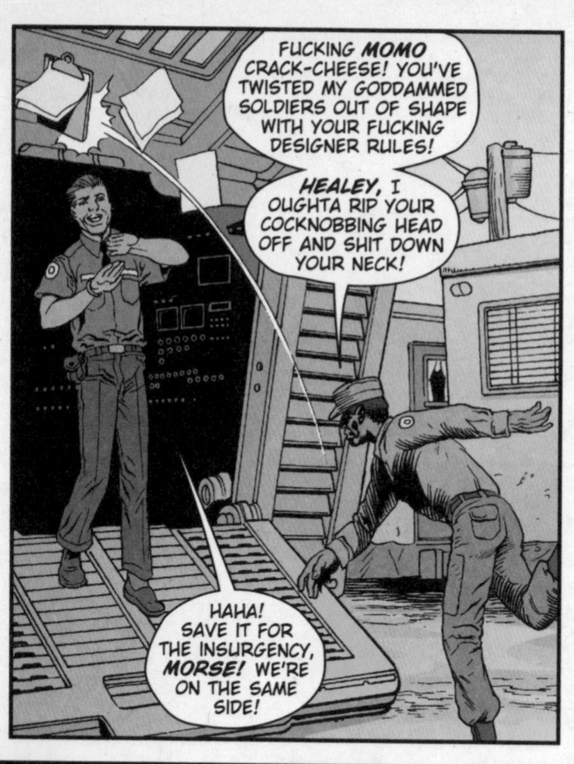

FUCKING MOMO CRACK-CHEESE! YOU'VE TWISTED MY GODDAMMED SOLDIERS OUT OF SHAPE WITH YOUR FUCKING DESIGNER RULES!
HEALEY, I OUGHTA RIP YOUR COCKNOBBING HEAD OFF AND SHIT DOWN YOUR NECK!
HAHA! SAVE IT FOR THE INSURGENCY, MORSE! WE'RE ON THE SAME SIDE!

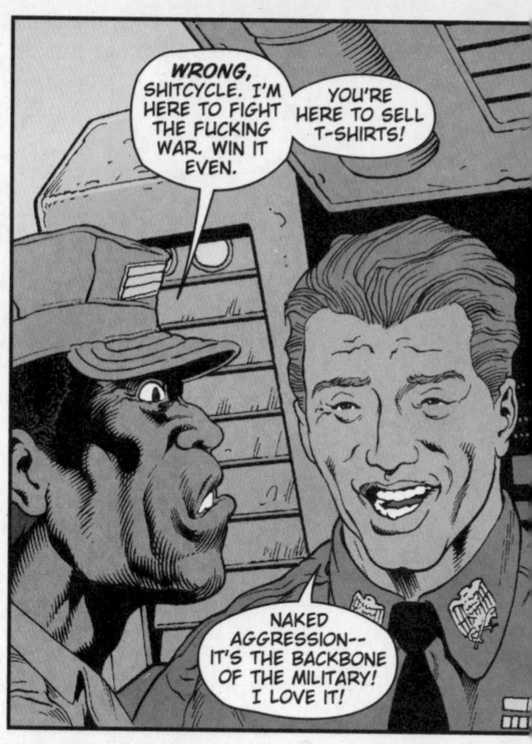

WRONG, SHITCYCLE. I'M HERE TO FIGHT THE FUCKING WAR. WIN IT EVEN.
YOU'RE HERE TO SELL T-SHIRTS!
NAKED AGGRESSION-- IT'S THE BACKBONE OF THE MILITARY! I LOVE IT!

LISTEN--SERIOUSLY NOW. DEE DEE GEST SHOWED UP AT MY SUITE BACK AT THE RESORT.
AND I BET SHE WASN'T LOOKING TO PUT LIPSTICK TO YOUR DIPSTICK EITHER.
NO SHE WASN'T. BUT SHE ACTUALLY MADE A TERRIFIC POINT ABOUT THE MEDIA POSSIBILITIES THAT WOULD OPEN UP IF BEAU IS AWARDED THE BRONZE STAR...

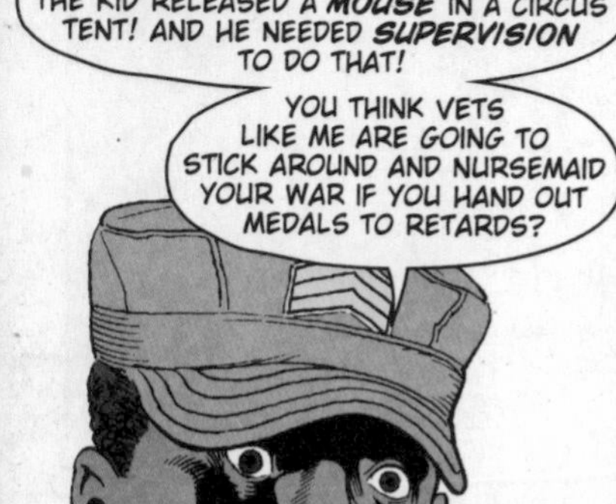

JESUS FUCKING WEPT, HEALEY! THE KID RELEASED A MOUSE IN A CIRCUS TENT! AND HE NEEDED SUPERVISION TO DO THAT!
YOU THINK VETS LIKE ME ARE GOING TO STICK AROUND AND NURSEMAID YOUR WAR IF YOU HAND OUT MEDALS TO RETARDS?

MORSE--REFERRING TO A DEVELOPMENTALLY DISABLED TROOPER BY THAT DEROGATORY TERM CAN GET YOU CASHIERED OVERNIGHT.
I OUGHT TO WARN YOU THAT DEE DEE IS THREATENING TO FILE CHARGES. AND NOW I'D HAVE TO TESTIFY...
WATCH IT! THAT'S MY FUCKIN RETIREMENT YOU' FUCKING WITH, HEALEY!

I'VE GOT YOUR BACK HERE, M'MAN. DEE DEE AND I HAD A DISCUSSION. WE CAME TO AN UNDERSTANDING.
SHE'LL DROP THE COMPLAINT IF YOU JUST LEND HER A COUPLE TROOPERS FOR A LITTLE JOB.
WHAT KIND OF JOB?

I DON'T KNOW AND I DON'T WANT TO KNOW. IT'S OFF THE BOOKS.
ARE YOU OUT OF YOUR FUCKING TREE? I CAN'T COMMIT MY PEOPLE TO THAT WOMAN'S AGENDA!
SHE'S GOT HER FINGER IN EVERY PILE OF CAMEL DUNG IN AFBAGHISTAN!

SHE'S ALSO GOT YOU BY THE GOOLIES, MORSE. AND YOU KNOW WHAT? SHE'LL NEVER LET GO.
MY ADVICE IS JUST GIVE HER WHATEVER SHE WANTS. I MEAN, WHAT CAN IT MATTER?
IF SOMEBODY DOESN'T STAND UP TO HER KIND OF BULLSHIT, THIS WHOLE THING BECOMES A FUCKING JOKE. THAT'S WHAT MATTERS!

WHAT? YOU'RE GOING TO SAY NO TO HER?
GIMME A BREAK.
WATCH ME, PECKERWOOD.

I'LL GIVE YOU A FUCKING BREAK, YOU FUCKING CORPORATE CRACK DEALER!
GRUNNNGRUUNNN
WE'LL BE SETTIN' OUT FOR HEAVEN IN MY LITTLE SPEED BOAT...
HEY! A CALL! IT'S FOR ME!
OH, HI, MOM! I'M DOING GOOD. UH-HUH. UH-HUH.
SERGEANT MORSE? HE'S RIGHT HERE...

HELLO, MRS. GEST. IF THIS IS ABOUT...
THAT'S EXACTLY WHAT IT'S ABOUT, SERGEANT.
I REQUIRE TWO OF YOUR BEST MEN FOR A FIVE-DAY ARMED EXCURSION. NO QUESTIONS ASKED.

I GOT IT WITH ME. TWO HUNDRED GRAND. IT'S ALL YOURS, SIS.

AND THANKS FOR HELPIN' ME OUT HERE. I MEAN IT. I REALLY APPRECIATE IT. REALLY.

YEAH. PICK ME UP AT THE WIFE'S TRAILER.

SNIK

HEY, HONEY. YOU AWAKE?

NOT NOWWW, BABE. I'VE GOT AN 0:500 REVEILLE.

WHAT--
I WORE YOU *OUT?*
LISTEN, UHH... I'M GONNA SPLIT. I GOT A LEAD ON *ALLIE.* I WANNA TRY AND FOLLOW IT UP.
MMHMM. SO WHERE IS SHE?

AHH, SOMEPLACE. I DUNNO.
YOU KEEP IT WIPED, EH? I'LL CATCH YOU LATER.
WHEN YOU COMING BACK?

I FIGURE AFTER I FIND HER, I'LL BEAT HOME TO EDGEFIELD.
I'M KIND OF A THIRD WHEEL AROUND HERE, ANYWAY.

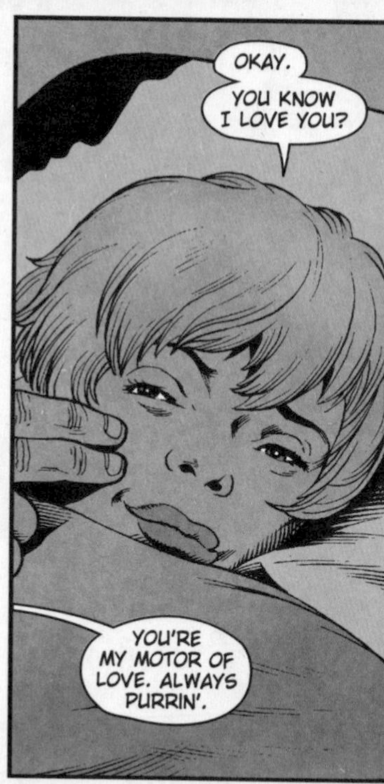
OKAY.
YOU KNOW I LOVE YOU?
YOU'RE MY MOTOR OF LOVE. ALWAYS PURRIN'.

UMM, HEY--ABOUT THAT MAGICIAN GUY? HE'S, LIKE, JUST A LITTLE FUN THING, RIGHT?
YOU'RE NOT, Y'KNOW-- REALLY GETTING *INTO* HIM OR...?

I-I'M NOT SO SURE...
...WHAT'S GOING ON WITH ME, RIGHT NOW, BABE.

THERE'S MY RIDE.
LISTEN, UHHHHH...CAN WE PICK THIS UP BACK HOME? YOU GOT FURLOUGH COMING UP, RIGHT?
I HAVE TO CHECK THE CALENDAR.

DON'T DO ANYTHING STUPID. OKAY, BABE?
HEY, YOU KNOW ME.
I'M AN ALLEYCAT.

GOT THE BEANS?
TWO HUNDRED GRAND. SHOULD GO A LONG WAY TO HELPING BEAU.
HERE. I WANT YOU TO COUNT IT.

IF THIS IS COUNTERFEIT...
NOT. THESE ARE NICE THOUSAND-DOLLAR PACKETS OF LIGHTLY CIRCULATED FIFTIES.
SEVENTEEN. EIGHTEEN. NINETEEN. TWENTY. SEE?

EVERY CENT I GOT.
SWEAR TO GOD.
YEAH, LOMAN. AND PIGS FLY.

RAJAH ISLAND, GULF OF AMHEN

MAGOON! HAVE YOU GOT THOSE **HOT ZONE** FILES READY?

Gimme gimme, ooh ooh.

I'M MEETING **SECRETARY STELAPHANE** IN TWENTY MINUTES!

THE COLONEL GOT CALLED BACK TO DEAL WITH MORE OF **DEE DEE'S** INSANITY SO I'M...

Gimme gimme, ooh ah.

Gimme gimme, ooh ooh.

WHAT'S THE MATTER? GOT SOMETHING STUCK IN YOUR THROAT?

Gimme gimme, ooh ooh.

DO YOU NEED ME TO APPLY THE HEIMLICH MANEUVER?

WELL, LOOK AT **THIS!** MISTER WANNABE ROCKSTAR, HIGHER THAN THE INTER-ORBITAL ASSASSINATION ARRAY!

MAGOON, YOU LOOK LIKE YOU'VE BLOWN RIGHT PAST THE STONED-OUT-OF-GOURD STAGE AND ARE FAST APPROACHING PERMANENT-BRAIN-DAMAGE.

I SUPPOSE I SHOULD FIGURE OUT WHAT YOU'VE BLITZED YOURSELF ON.

Gimme gimme, ooh ooh. Gimme gimme, ooh ah.

EXTADRINE! YOU TOOK FOUR OF THESE THINGS?
Gimme gimme, ooh ooh.
THIS IS HEAVY STUFF! PSYCHE GUYS USE IT TO PROGRAM BIG FINGER; BUT THEY GET YEARS OF TRAINING.

Gimme gimme, ooh ah.
THESE PACK ENOUGH UPPERS, DOWNERS, INNERS AND OUTERS TO TURN A CHAMELEON PERMANENTLY PLAID.
BUT IT'S THE BUILT-IN WIFI IN EACH CAPSULE THAT NETWORKS THE USER TO BIG FINGER.
SO THE SIMPLEST WAY TO DISCONNECT YOU IS A STOMACH PUMP.

AND EVERY GOOD SECRETARY KNOWS THE QUICKEST WAY TO DO THAT IS CALL 911.
I'LL JUST USE YOUR LAPTOP.
JEEZ, WHAT WERE YOU WATCHING? THESE TWO PEOPLE LOOK LIKE...

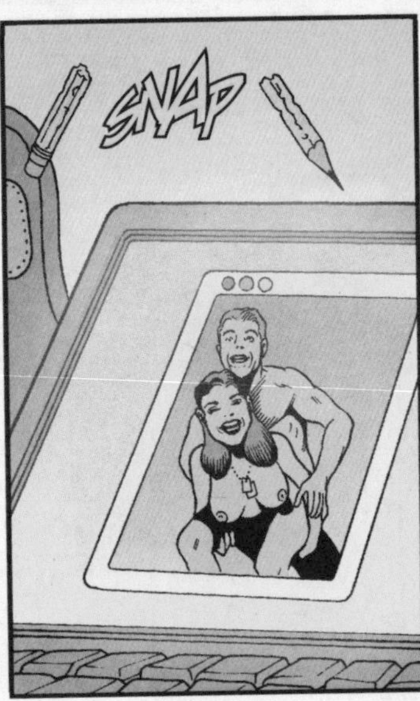
SNAP

FOR THIS...
Ptoo!
...PAYBACK WILL BE A MOTHERFUCKER.

WHAT DOES THE GOOD SECRETARY ALWAYS KEEP IN HER SATCHEL? WHY, IT'S A HANDY DANDY TUBE OF SUPER GLUE!
A FEW DABS PLACED IN JUST THE RIGHT LOCATION CREATES AN UNBREAKABLE BOND!
Gimme gimme, ooh ooh.

Gimme gimme, ooh ah.
SO MR. WANNABE ROCKSTAR NEED NEVER BE SEPARATED FROM HIS INSTRUMENT. EVER AGAIN!
NOW, WHAT ELSE DOES THE GOOD SECRETARY HAVE IN HER BAG OF TRICKS?
SPOONT

OOOOH? HAIR STYLING TOOLS!
I WONDER WHAT I CAN DO WITH THESE?
Gimme gimme, ooh asooh.

EXCUSE ME, LIEUTENANT WOYNER. YOUR LAUNCH IS READY.
BE RIGHT WITH YOU, MAJOR FRICK. JUST FINISHING UP A LITTLE STYLING JOB.
NICE, HUH?
Gimme gimme, ooh ah.
IT'S REFRESHING TO SEE THE MILITARY ALLOWING MORE DIVERSITY IN PERSONAL GROOMING STYLES.
IT REALLY IS, ISN'T IT?
LISTEN, I'VE GOT ONE MORE TASK I NEED TO ACCOMPLISH.
Polka Cola
Polk
I JUST HAVE TO SWAP OUT THE HARD DRIVE ON THIS LAPTOP.
Gimme gimme, ooh ah.
NO RUSH.
TAKE YOUR TIME.
Gimme gimme, ooh ooh.
Polk
THAT LITTLE DITTY LIEUTENANT MAGOON WAS SINGING SOUNDED STRANGELY FAMILIAR. DO YOU KNOW WHAT IT'S FROM?
NO. BUT IT WAS KIND OF CATCHY, WASN'T IT?
VRRR
LIEUTENANT WOYNER, SIR.
PERMISSION TO COME ABOARD, SECRETARY STELAPHANE?
YOU MAY TAKE TWO GIANT STEPS!
AND LET ME SAY HOW ABSOLUTELY DELIGHTED I AM THAT COLONEL HEALEY HAD TO SEND YOU IN HIS PLACE TODAY.

YOU'RE SOMEONE I CAN DO BUSINESS WITH, LIEUTENANT. AND DAMMIT, I'M READY FOR A MIMOSA!
WHAT WOULD YOU LIKE, LIEUTENANT??
ALCOHOL ON DUTY, SIR?
LISTEN. WE BOTH KNOW WHO PUT THE POLKA COLA SPONSORSHIP DEAL TOGETHER. AND WHAT IT MEANS TO ME, PERSONALLY.
YOU'RE A MOVER AND A SHAKER IN THIS WAR, LIEUTENANT. MIGHT AS WELL FACE UP TO IT AND ENJOY THE PERKS.
IN THAT CASE, I'LL HAVE A ZOMBIE WOOF, MAJOR.
I'M HAPPY TO REPORT WE'VE BEEN BUSY AT MOTIVATION & MORALE, SIR. WHERE WOULD YOU LIKE TO START?
I THINK WE START WITH ME GOING INTO CARDIAC ARREST. FOLLOWED BY YOU APPLYING MOUTH-TO-MOUTH RESUSCITATION. FOLLOWED BY ME...
SORRY. EVERY ONCE IN A WHILE MY ID CREATURE ESCAPES AND RUNS AMOK.
SO IT SAYS IN YOUR REPORT THERE'S NOW A WAIT LIST TO JOIN THE MILITARY? WITH SOME PEOPLE SELLING THEIR PLACES IN LINE ON EBAY?
THE HOT ZONE CLUB'S RECRUITING POTENTIAL IS PROVING BOTTOMLESS, SIR.
WE'VE GOT ALL OUR CORPORATE ASSETS INJECTING THE HOT ZONE VIRUS INTO THE THE MEDIA-STREAM.
THE TRICK TO AVOID SCANDAL IS TO KEEP IT SUBLIMINAL. WE WANT OUR TARGET CONSUMERS TO RESPOND TO THE SIREN CALL JUST BELOW THE LEVEL OF AWARENESS.
BUT IT SAYS HERE YOU ARE NOT CONCERNED ABOUT THAT RETREAT VIDEO BIG FINGER DISCOVERED ON THE NET?
SIR, I'VE RUN NUMEROUS CHECKS, BACKWARDS AND FORWARDS. I AM WILLING TO BET MY UTERUS THERE WAS NO VIDEO LEAKED FROM ANY RETREAT.
NICELY ARTICULATED. I LIKE THAT. AND I LIKE YOU.
SO I'M GOING TO SHARE MY NEWEST PROBLEM WITH YOU. IT HAS TO DO WITH BIG FINGER...
Polka Cola

AS YOU KNOW, BIG FINGER BEGAN AS A META-PROGRAM SIFTING THE DATA IT INHALED FROM EVERY NODULE ON THE NET.
AT THIS POINT THE PROGRAM HAS GROWN SO FAR-REACHING AND COMPLEX THAT IT'S NOT CLASSIFIED AS AN ARTIFICIAL INTELLIGENCE ANYMORE.
WE'RE ESSENTIALLY DEALING WITH A PSYCHOLOGICAL ENTITY.
ANYONE WHO EVER WATCHED SATURDAY MORNING CARTOONS CAN GRASP THAT CONCEPT, SIR.
LET ME ASK YOU, MR. SECRETARY: WHERE DOES BIG FINGER THINK THE VIDEO CAME FROM?
BIG FINGER NOW SAYS THAT THE DIGITAL INFORMATION ON OUR VIDEO WAS NOT GENERATED IN THIS SPACETIME.
BIG FINGER IS CONVINCED THAT IT WAS TRANSMITTED TO US FROM SOME FUTURE SPACETIME.
AH. AND FROM THAT YOU CAN ONLY ASSUME THAT (A) BIG FINGER IS WRONG.
OR (B)...
BIG FINGER IS RIGHT.
SEE, YOU'VE GOT THE NOSE FOR THIS. YOU'VE PINPOINTED EXACTLY WHERE THINGS GET INTERESTING.
VERY PERCEPTIVE.
AND EITHER WAY IT CUTS...
WE'VE GOT ONE HELL OF A STRATEGIC PROBLEM.
I'M SORRY TO DISTURB YOU, SIR.
ITS POMONA PEEBLES ON THE PHONE. SHE'S ABSOLUTELY ADAMANT ABOUT SEEING YOU.
TELL THAT SAGGING SILICON QUEEN I'M BUSY!

HE'S TRYING TO HIDE FROM ME.
BUT AT LEAST NOW I KNOW HE'S ON HIS FAT-ASS YACHT!
YOUR FEELINGS ARE HURT BECAUSE YOUR GENTLEMAN FRIEND WILL NOT SEE YOU?
WAKE UP! WITHOUT STELAPHANE I CAN'T FLY CARS INTO AFBAGHISTAN.
AND WITHOUT CARS WHERE DOES THAT LEAVE ME?
NOT STUCK IN TRAFFIC?
NO. IT LEAVES ME JUST LIKE YOU.
SELLING MY ASS INTO BONDAGE TO MAKE MY DAILY SALT.
I HAVE ACCEPTED THE YOKE OF SERVITUDE NOT FOR SELFISH PROFIT, BUT FOR MY FAMILY'S HONOR.
HEY-- DON'T KNOCK SELFISHNESS. WITHOUT IT, I WOULDN'T HAVE A BOAT TO ROW HOME IN!
WHICH GIVES ME AN IDEA ON HOW TO GET STELAPHANE TO PAY ATTENTION TO ME.
HOW ARE YOU WITH A SAIL AND A STIFF WIND?
BVOOOM
OH SHIT! WHAT NOW?
BOMB IN THE TOLLBOOTH!

THERE WILL BE CASUALTIES! I MUST GO HELP.
ARE YOU CRAZY? GET YOUR ASS BACK IN HERE!
AND WE'LL BE SETTIN' OUT FOR HEAVEN IN MY LITTLE SPEED BOAT...
OH MY GOD! IT'S DADDY! I'VE GOT TO TAKE THIS!

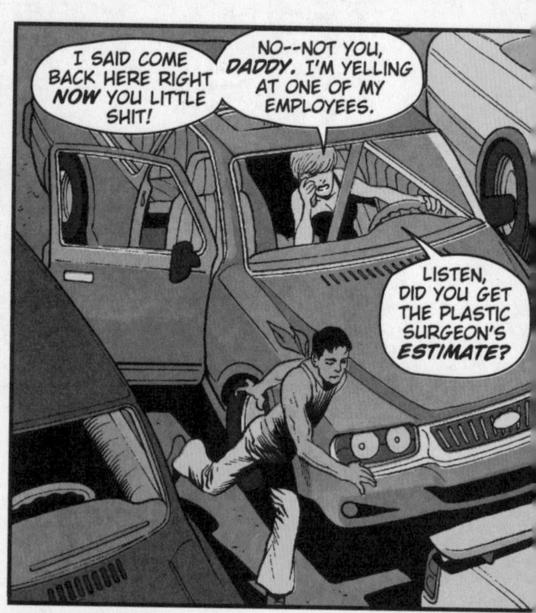
I SAID COME BACK HERE RIGHT NOW YOU LITTLE SHIT!
NO--NOT YOU, DADDY. I'M YELLING AT ONE OF MY EMPLOYEES.
LISTEN, DID YOU GET THE PLASTIC SURGEON'S ESTIMATE?

I DID. AND I GOTTA SAY I WISH I'D SENT YOU TO MED SCHOOL INSTEAD OF TEACHING YOU TO SELL CARS.
TWO HUNDRED AND FIFTY GRAND FOR A BOOB JOB? WHAT ARE THEY PUTTIN' IN, SOLID GOLD NIPPLES?

DADDY, PLEEEASE. I'M STARTING TO SAG AND PEOPLE ARE NOTICING. I REEALLY NEEED AUGMENTATION.
AND THIS GUY DID LUSH RIMBAUD'S SEX CHANGE!
OKAY, I'M IMPRESSED. I'LL PUT UP THE CASH.

BUT IT'S COMING OUT OF YOUR BACK END. AND NEED I REMIND YOU THERE WILL BE NO BACK END UNLESS YOU GET ANOTHER PLANELOAD OF CARS INTO THE BAGH?
MOVE THOSE UNITS! DO WHATEVER YOU HAVE TO! GOT IT?

I'M NOT RUNNING A CHARITY HERE.
Y-YES, DADDY.

I GET IT.

CAN YOU BELIEVE IT? MORSE PICKED US TO GO ON A HUSH-HUSH MISSION!
WE HAVE PROOF POSITIVE THE LOVE SPELL HAS BEEN LIFTED, FLABB-DUDE!
Y'KNOW, YOU MAY BE RIGHT, ROYDEN.
I AM FEELING A LITTLE MORE LIKE MY OLD SELF.
THE MAGIC MONKEY HAS BROUGHT OUR UNIT'S BIGGEST PARTY ANIMAL BACK FROM THE LIVING DEAD!
YEAH. FOR THE FIRST TIME IN MONTHS, MY THOUGHTS ARE CLEAR OF SWITZER.
THE WHOLE PROBLEM REALLY WAS THIS STUPID WICCAN CHARM.
I CAN'T BELIEVE I FELL UNDER ITS POWER OF SUGGESTION.
AND ME-- A TRAINED HYPNOTIST! SHEEESH!
IT'S TIME TO CONSIGN LITTLE MISS SWITZER TO THE TRASHCAN OF MY ROMANTIC HISTORY.
LET'S ROCK, FLAB!
HOO-AH! HOO-AH!

TROOPERS FLABBERGAST AND ROYDEN REPORTING FOR COMBAT DUTY, SAR'NT!
WE'RE READY TO SLICE, DICE, CHOP AND PUREE!
GENTLEMEN. I LIKE THE ATTITUDE.

REQUEST TO TAKE MY MAGIC MONKEY ON THE MISSION, SAR'NT?
HE'S OUR GOOD LUCK CHARM!
WHY NOT? JUST MAKE SURE IT TAKES A RUNNY DUMP ON DEE DEE GEST'S HEAD FOR ME.

BEAU'S GONNA SNAP YOUR PICTURE WITH HIS PHONE, FLAB. GIVE US THOSE BEDROOM EYES!
HI, LADIES!
FRONT AND CENTER. HERE'S YOUR RIDE.
HELLO, MY BEAUTIFUL BOY!

LISTEN, I'D JUST LIKE TO KNOW WHERE THEY'RE GOING IN CASE ANYTHING...
WHAT PART OF "NO QUESTIONS" DO YOU NOT UNDERSTAND, SERGEANT?

OKAY. DO WHATEVER SHE SAYS, BUT GET YOUR ASSES BACK IN ONE PIECE.
TRUST ME, SAR'NT. I GOT MY GAME BACK.
AND WE'LL BE SETTIN' OUT FOR HEAVEN IN MY LITTLE SPEED BOAT...

UHHH...
UHHH...

HI! MY NAME'S POOKIE PYEWACKET! WHAT'S YOURS?
I'M BEAU.
WHAT A LOVELY NAME. I'D LIKE TO GET TO KNOW YOU BETTER, BEAU. WOULD YOU LIKE TO KNOW ME BETTER?
UH HUH.

IF YOU JOIN MY FANTASY PHONE DATING GAME, WE CAN BE FRIENDS. IT'S FUN AND SO MUCH MORE.
TO ACCEPT A ONE-MONTH FREE TRIAL, JUST PRESS 1. WE CAN BEGIN TALKING AND GETTING TO KNOW EACH OTHER RIGHT NOW.

CAN I DO IT, SERGEANT? PLEASE? PLEASE?
WHAT IS THIS? SOME SORT OF SEX THING?
HEY, SWITZER! YOU KNOW ANYTHING ABOUT THIS PHONE SHIT?

IT'S A DATING SIMULATOR, SAR'NT. YOU TALK TO A CHARACTER AND THE ARTIFICIAL INTELLIGENCE PROGRAM AUTOMATICALLY ANSWERS BACK. IT MIGHT BE GOOD FOR BEAU.
AND IF IT'S ON THE ENCRYPTED NETWORK IT MUST BE SAFE.

SAY, UH, YOU HAVEN'T SEEN FLABBERGAST AROUND, HAVE YOU, SAR'NT?
HIM? NAH. HE GOT CALLED AWAY. ONE OF HIS MAGICIAN THINGS. DUNNO WHEN HE'LL BE BACK.

WHY YOU OUT DOGGING THIS LATE AT NIGHT?
YOU GOT 0:500 REVEILLE TOMORROW.
OKAY, SAR'NT. I'M GOING. G'NIGHT.
HELLO, POOKIE? I CAN DO IT!

I'M PUSHING THE BUTTON.
OH! OOOHHH! I'VE NEVER FELT ANYTHING SO... WONDERFUL!
THANK YOU, BEAU.
PERHAPS YOU ARE MY REAL PRINCE CHARMING?

BATSUKH? FEEL LIKE TALKING?
Mmmm.
THE MOON IS INCREDIBLE.

WHEN YOU TOLD ME I WAS, LIKE, RADIANT WITH INNER LIGHT? THAT'S THE MOST BEAUTIFUL THING ANYONE EVER SAID TO ME.
I MEAN, MY OLD HUSBAND USED TO SAY THINGS, LIKE I WAS HIS GODDESS.
AND I WANTED TO BELIEVE HIM. BUT HE WASN'T...

...REAL?

Cooooo...

Puurrrrrrr

B-BUH-BATSUKH! IT'S HER! THE MOTHER! SHE'S HERE!
WAKE UP! WAKE UP!
HMMM?

READY FOR ANOTHER MOONDANCE, MY LOVE?
WHA...?
YOU'RE MY GODDESS, **ALLIE.** MY PERSONAL APHRODITE!
WAIT! NO. THIS ISN'T RIGHT.
I'M **MARRIED.**
OF COURSE WE ARE, MY DARLING!
YOU AND I, TOGETHER. FOREVER AND EVER!
NO. **NO!** I BELONG TO **BATSUKH!**
BATSUKH!!

BANGDAGONG PROVINCE, AFBAGHISTAN-MONGROLIAN BORDER
SOMETHIN' ABOUT MONSTERS, MAN.
EVEN AFTER FRANKENSTEIN STRANGLES THE LITTLE KID, Y'GOTTA, LIKE, SYMPATHIZE WITH HIM. Y'KNOW?
A FEW YEARS IN THE FUTURE.
ME, I'M MORE OF A TEENAGE WOLFMAN GUY MYSELF.
FIRST TIME I SAW THAT WAS RIGHT AFTER A MARATHON WEEKEND OF LITTLE HOUSE ON THE PRAIRIE.
I WAS, LIKE... THREE.
WHEN YOUNG PA STARTED GROWING HAIR AND FANGS IT SCARED THE HOT BUBBLING BLUEBERRIES RIGHT OUT OF ME.
THAT'S IT. UP AHEAD.
ANYWAY, THAT'S WHY I LOVE MONSTERS.
THAT'S GOOD, ROYDEN.
BECAUSE YOU'RE GOING TO REALLY GET YOUR ROCKS OFF ON THIS.

NO WAY!
YEAH, WAY.
SEVEN LEAGUE BOOTS
THERE'S R&D REJECTS LIKE THIS STASHED ALL OVER THE COUNTRY. MOST OF IT NEVER PICKED UP A SPONSORSHIP.
I SAW THESE IN POPULAR MECHANICALS. THEY'RE CALLED EXO-SUITS.
YOU CAN MARCH, LIKE, SIX HUNDRED MILES A DAY IN 'EM.
I DON'T LIKE THE SMELL OF THIS, ROYDEN.
ARE YOU SHITTIN' ME? WE'RE GONNA BE LIKE RIPLEY FIGHTING BIG MAMA ALIEN!
YOU HAVEN'T LOST YOUR MOJO AGAIN, HAVE YOU, FLAB?

THIS MULE COMES WITH EVERYTHING YOU'LL NEED. IT CONTROLS THE WHOLE SYSTEM.
ONCE I PROGRAM IN THE GPS COORDINATES IT'LL DELIVER YOU RIGHT TO ALLIE'S DOORSTEP.
SIS, YOU ARE INCREDIBLE. I DON'T KNOW HOW I--
DON'T WASTE YOUR BREATH, LOMAN. THIS IS BUSINESS. SPEAKING OF WHICH...

GOTCHA COVERED. HERE. I HOPE IT HELPS.
SO I GOTTA ASK, WHAT IS IT WITH YOU AND ALLIE ANYWAY?

NUTHIN' TO WORRY ABOUT.
LISTEN. I KNOW I'VE BEEN AN ASSHOLE A COUPLE TIMES.
I JUST WANT TO THANK YOU FOR, Y'KNOW...BEIN' MY SISTER.
REALLY.

WHATEVER HAPPENS, YOU TAKE GOOD CARE OF BEAU, HUH? HE'S THE ONLY NEPHEW I GOT.
JUST DON'T GET YOUR HEAD BLOWN OFF.
OKAY?

HEY, YOU KNOW ME.
I'M AN ALLEY CAT.

OKAY, SO HOW DO I STEER THIS THING?
YOU DON'T.
ALL THE NEW SHIT RUNS ITSELF. ALL WE DO IS POINT AND GO!

WOAH! THIS THING MOVES LIKE A GODDAMN BALLET DANCER!
YOUR TAX DOLLARS AT WORK.
HOO-AH!
FUCKING ACE, MAN!

MAYBE I WAS A LITTLE TOO COLD WITH ***LOMAN.*** HE HAD SUCH A HARD TIME GROWING UP.
OUR DAD USED TO BEAT THE CRAP OUT OF HIM.
HEY, DID YOU COUNT THIS MONEY?

I ***THOUGHT*** I DID.
NO, WAIT. I ONLY COUNTED ONE BUNDLE. THE OTHERS HE FLASHED AT ME.
REAL BILLS ON TOP. THE REST ARE BLANKS.

THAT FUCKING WEASEL SON OF A--

SINKYANG FRONTIER
OUTER MONGROLIAN REPUBLIC
MY PEOPLE HAVE BEEN HORSEMEN SINCE TIME IMMEMORIAL.
WHISPERING IS OUR WAY OF COMMUNICATING WITH THE ANIMALS. AND WITH EACH OTHER.
I COULD NEVER DO ANYTHING LIKE THAT, BATSUKH.
YOUR CARESSES TELL ME JUST THE OPPOSITE, ALLIE.
ALL I'M TALENTED AT IS SHOPPING. AND MAYBE WHINING ABOUT MY DUMB HUSBAND.
THESE BEAUTIFUL HANDS ARE POWERFUL SENSORY ORGANS!
CLOSE YOUR EYES AND LET MONGOL'S ESSENCE PULSE BENEATH YOUR FINGERS.
OOOH. THERE'S SUCH A...LOYALTY.
MONGOL WOULD DIE FOR YOU, BATSUKH.
THAT HE WOULD.
NOW LET ME SHOW YOU HOW A PERSON MIGHT PLACE A MESSAGE INSIDE THE ANIMAL...
Huaalp!
SORRY. KOF TUMMY'S UPSET.
STILL HAVING ISSUES WITH YOUR WEIGHT, ALLIE?
NO...KOF. NOT THAT. I'VE JUST PICKED UP A STOMACH BUG OR SOMETHING.
I'VE THROWN UP THE LAST COUPLE MORNINGS.

ACTUALLY, I COULD GO FOR ANOTHER HEAPING HELPING OF OUR WEDDING STEW RIGHT NOW.
AND WHAT COMES AFTER TOO!
HAHA! THEN LET ME BE YOUR LOYAL STEED!
THERE'S NOT MUCH STEW LEFT, I'M AFRAID. WHEN IT IS GONE, IT WILL BE TIME TO RETURN TO THE YURT.
AND I'LL HAVE TO DECIDE WHETHER OR NOT I WANT TO SIGN ON TO A LIFE OF SQUALOR AND BIGAMY, HUH?
IS THERE ANY DOUBT?
ABOUT WHAT I'M FEELING? NO.
I HAVEN'T HAD A COMB THROUGH MY HAIR IN OVER A WEEK. I'VE PUT ON AT LEAST FIVE POUNDS. BUT SOMEHOW IT DOESN'T MATTER.
INSTEAD, ALL I THINK OF IS YOU. EVERYTHING YOU SAY, EVERYTHING YOU DO HAS THIS SOULFUL DEPTH THAT JUST FASCINATES ME.
BUT YOU HAVE TO UNDERSTAND HOW I'VE BEEN LIED TO. I'VE GOT THESE SELF-ESTEEM PROBLEMS-- YOU KNOW?
I WANT TO TRUST YOU, BATSUKH. I DO! IT'S JUST THAT...
I'M NOT SURE, AFTER ALL THE OTHERS, I EVEN KNOW HOW ANYMORE.
I HAVE FOUR OTHER WIVES, EACH OF WHOM I LOVE AS THE SUN DOES THE VERDANT EARTH.
YET NONE ARE AS INTOXICATING... AS YOU.
JOIN US, ALLIE. YOU SHALL ALWAYS BE MY FAVORITE.
OH GOD! YES BATSUKH.
YES!

REEEAAAAGGHH!
BREEAUOOGHH
IS THAT SOME SORT OF WOUNDED ANIMAL?
NO--IT'S THE MOTHER OF MOUNTAIN. AND THIS TIME WE'RE NOT DREAMING!
BLEAUUGHWW! BLEEEAUURGH!
SHE HAS A MESSAGE FOR US.
I-IS IT POSSIBLE TO TALK TO A CREATURE LIKE THAT?
THE ONLY WAY TO ENGAGE THE MOTHER IS TO SEND AN EMISSARY FROM THE ANIMAL WORLD.
MONGOL WILL CARRY MOTHER OF MOUNTAIN'S MESSAGE.
HE'S TERRIFIED, BATSUKH. I CAN FEEL IT.
WHO WOULDN'T BE?

IDI-AMIN PROVINCE, AFBAGHISTAN
HELLO, POOKIE? THIS IS BEAU.
I'M ON BREAK SO I'M CALLING TO SEE HOW YOU ARE DOING.
YOU OKAY?
I'M SO HAPPY TO HEAR YOUR VOICE!
I'M DOING WONDERFULLY EXCEPT... EXCEPT...
OF COURSE! IT'S JUST THAT THERE'S ONE SPECIAL THING I'VE BEEN WISHING FOR.

I WOULD LOVE A PICTURE OF YOU.
PLEASE SEND ME A GOOD PHOTO SO I CAN SEE WHAT MY PRINCE CHARMING LOOKS LIKE.
UHHHH, I DON'T KNOW...
IT'S NORMAL WHEN PEOPLE LIKE EACH OTHER THAT THEY SHARE PHOTOS, BEAU. DON'T YOU LIKE ME?
Uh...uh...uh. I GOTTA GO. I GOTTA...
KLIK

IDIOT! YOU'VE LOST HIM!
WHOP
UNGHCH!!
HOW MANY TIMES DO I HAVE TO TELL YOU? YOU MUST THINK LIKE A CARTOON FANTASY!
NOT A REAL WOMAN!
THE FAULT IS... ENTIRELY MINE, COLONEL. I WIL WORK DILIGENTLY TO REGAIN HIS TRUST.

HEYYA, BEAU. HOW'S THE NEW HONEY-PIE TREATING YOU?
GOT TO FIRST BASE YET?
AWWW. I CAN'T CALL POOKIE NO MORE, SWITZER.
WHAT DO YOU MEAN? YOU JUST DIAL HER UP. THAT'S HOW IT, ER...
I MEAN, THAT'S HOW POOKIE WORKS.
YEAH, BUT NOW SHE REALLY WANTS MY PICTURE.
THEN SEND IT! SWAPPING PIX IS PART OF HOOKING UP.
I CAN'T BECAUSE SHE THINKS I'M HER PRINCE CHARMING.
AN' ONCE SHE SEES A PHOTO OF ME, WELL...
...SHE WON'T THINK THAT NO MORE.
BEAU, THIS IS NOT A PROBLEM. WE'LL SEND HER A PICTURE OF SOMEONE ELSE.
THAT'S NOT FAIR.
IN THIS WORLD THERE IS NO FAIR.
LET'S SEE WHOSE MUG YOU GOT ON HERE.
FLABBERGAST! THE PERFECT CANDIDATE.

GET OVER HERE.
YOU KNOW WHAT I WANT.
YOU DARE DISOBEY YOUR COMMANDING OFFICER?
I ORDER YOU! STRIP DOWN! ASSUME THE POSITION!
YES SIR.
NOT AGAIN, SIR. PLEASE, I...
YOU LOVE IT. YOU KNOW YOU...HUH?
HELLO, POOKY? UMMM, HEY-- THIS IS BEAU AGAIN.
ARE YOU THERE?
HELLO, BEAU! I-I'M SO HAPPY *Sniff* THAT YOU CALLED BACK.
HEY. YOU'RE CRYING.
WHAT'S THE MATTER? DID SOMEONE HURT YOU?
THANK YOU FOR BEING CONCERNED. I-IT MEANS A LOT RIGHT NOW.
BUT I'M ONLY SAD BECAUSE I HAVE NO PHOTO OF YOU.
BIG SURPRISE! I'M SENDING YOU MY PICTURE *Snicker* SO YOU CAN SEE WHAT I REALLY LOOK LIKE!
BOOP
Y-YES. IT'S COMING THROUGH.
AND YOU REALLY ARE...
...MY PRINCE CHARMING.

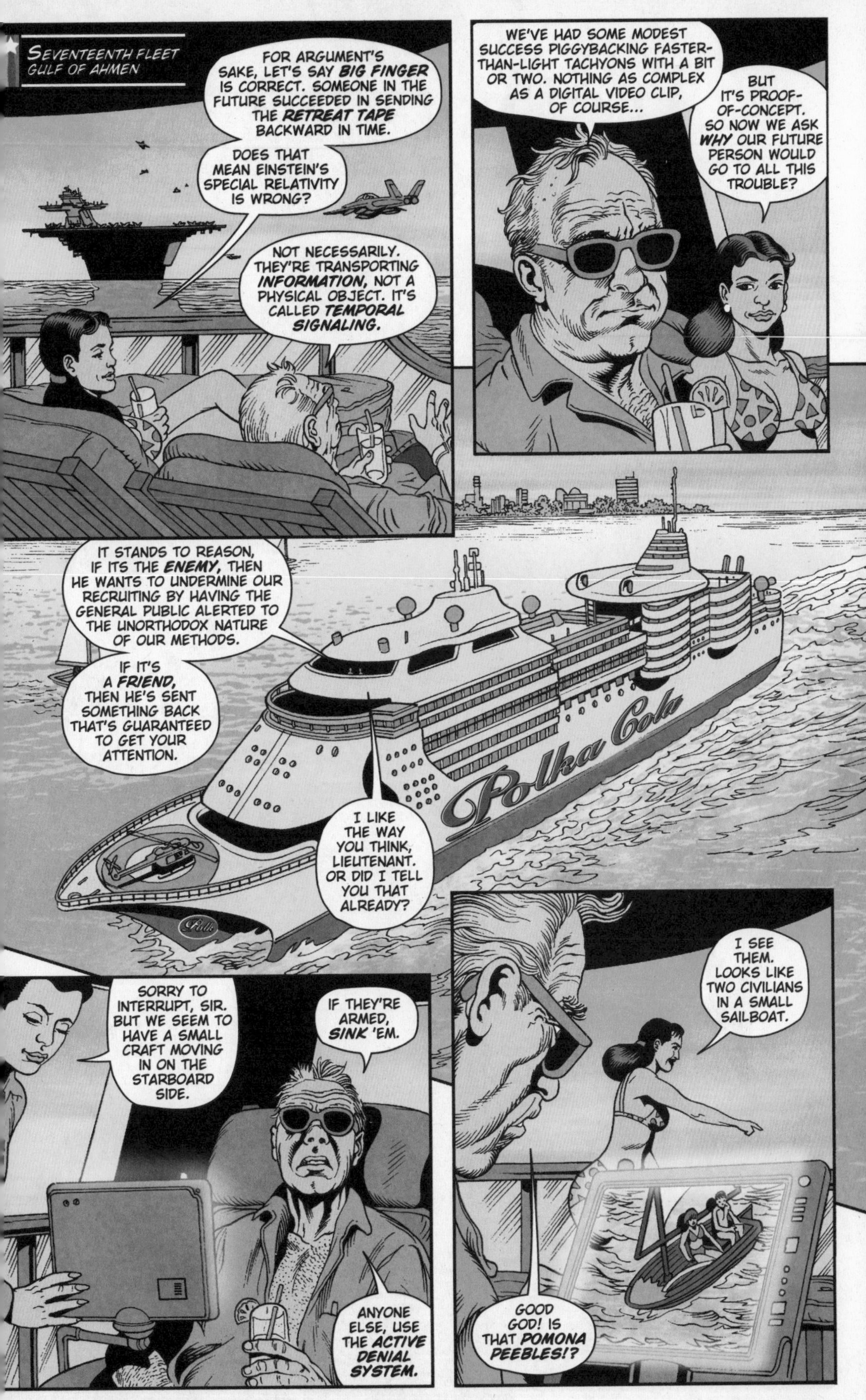
SEVENTEENTH FLEET
GULF OF AHMEN
FOR ARGUMENT'S SAKE, LET'S SAY BIG FINGER IS CORRECT. SOMEONE IN THE FUTURE SUCCEEDED IN SENDING THE RETREAT TAPE BACKWARD IN TIME.
DOES THAT MEAN EINSTEIN'S SPECIAL RELATIVITY IS WRONG?
NOT NECESSARILY. THEY'RE TRANSPORTING INFORMATION, NOT A PHYSICAL OBJECT. IT'S CALLED TEMPORAL SIGNALING.
WE'VE HAD SOME MODEST SUCCESS PIGGYBACKING FASTER-THAN-LIGHT TACHYONS WITH A BIT OR TWO. NOTHING AS COMPLEX AS A DIGITAL VIDEO CLIP, OF COURSE...
BUT IT'S PROOF-OF-CONCEPT. SO NOW WE ASK WHY OUR FUTURE PERSON WOULD GO TO ALL THIS TROUBLE?
IT STANDS TO REASON, IF ITS THE ENEMY, THEN HE WANTS TO UNDERMINE OUR RECRUITING BY HAVING THE GENERAL PUBLIC ALERTED TO THE UNORTHODOX NATURE OF OUR METHODS.
IF IT'S A FRIEND, THEN HE'S SENT SOMETHING BACK THAT'S GUARANTEED TO GET YOUR ATTENTION.
Polka Cola
I LIKE THE WAY YOU THINK, LIEUTENANT. OR DID I TELL YOU THAT ALREADY?
SORRY TO INTERRUPT, SIR. BUT WE SEEM TO HAVE A SMALL CRAFT MOVING IN ON THE STARBOARD SIDE.
IF THEY'RE ARMED, SINK 'EM.
ANYONE ELSE, USE THE ACTIVE DENIAL SYSTEM.
I SEE THEM. LOOKS LIKE TWO CIVILIANS IN A SMALL SAILBOAT.
GOOD GOD! IS THAT POMONA PEEBLES!?

Polka Dot
I'M NOT SURE IF IT IS WISE TO APPROACH A SHIP THIS SIZE, MISS POMONA.
YOU DON'T HAVE A VOTE, ISSA! MOVE IN CLOSER!
GET READY TO LOWER THE SAIL!
BUT IT'S THE ONLY WAY TO STEER!
TOUGH SHIT! I NEED THE MAST!
THE OLD POOPEROO WILL BE UP THERE WATCHING MY EVERY MOVE WITH HIS SPY TOYS!
WELL, I'M GOING TO GIVE HIM A SHOW HE WON'T HAVE ANY DEFENSE AGAINST.
TURN ON THE MUSIC! LOUD!
Y-YES, MA'AM.
WE'LL BE SETTIN' OUT FOR HEAVEN...
IS SHE POLE-DANCING OUT THERE?
I'M AFRAID SO.
...IN MY LITTLE SPEED BOAT!
WANT TO SEE HER REALLY DANCE? I'LL GIVE HER A SHOT OF OUR ACTIVE DENIAL SYSTEM ACROSS THE BOW.
WITH THE MICROWAVE SET HOT ENOUGH TO FRY AN EGG.
RMMRMMM
MY CHI CHI'S MAY NEED A LITTLE WORK, BUT MY BOOTY IS STILL WORLD CLASS.
THE SHIP'S WAKE--LOOK OUT!

URRRMMMMRMMRMMM
Hah?
SNAP
CRACKLE
POP

WAAAAH!
MY ASS!
MY ASS!
MY ASS IS ON FIRE!

I'VE GOT YOU, MISS POMONA.
A-ARE YOU INJURED?
I-I DON'T KNOW. SOMETHING FEELS KIND OF... WEIRD DOWN THERE.

I THINK MY BUTT IMPLANTS JUST...
...MELTED?

SO IF THIS ***TEMPORAL SIGNALING*** IS POSSIBLE...
...SHOULDN'T WE BE CONSIDERING OUR OPTIONS?
SUCH AS?

WELL, FOR STARTERS, WE COULD SIGNAL BACK.
QUITE EASILY, IN FACT.
YOU MEAN LEAVE A MESSAGE FOR OUR FUTURE PEN PAL TO FIND?

BUT, CONSIDERING THE INFINITE TSUNAMI OF INFORMATION AND DATA WE GENERATE EVERY MILLISECOND, ***WHERE*** WILL HE EVEN KNOW TO LOOK?
WELL. SIR, WE ALREADY KNOW HE HAS ACCESS TO THE ***RETREAT*** TAPES.
WE CAN HAVE MOMO INCLUDE TH RETURN MESSAGE THERE.
WHICH REMINDS ME. I SHOULD CHECK IN ON COLONEL ***HEALEY.***
Polk

HULLO.
HI, IT'S ***WOYNER.*** HOW YOU DOING?
FINE.
BUBEEP BOOP BOOP
YOU DON'T SOUND FINE. WHAT'S THE MATTER?

NOTHING.
TELL ME WHAT'S TROUBLING YOU, SIR. I'LL FIX IT.
YOU CAN'T.
PLEASE, SIR.
WELL...

I MISS ***ALLIE.***

SILK ROAD
LOWER MONGROLIA
IF WE KEEP TO MAIN ROADS LIKE THIS, WON'T WE END UP BEING SEEN?
THE SYSTEM'S GOT IT COVERED!
YEAH. IT'S OMNISCIENT FOR FIVE MILES IN ALL DIRECTIONS, MAN.
IT'S GOT A KEYBOARD AND ALL THESE MENUS ON SCREEN.
HOW'S ABOUT I TAKE IT OFF AUTO-PILOT? Y'KNOW--DRIVE THE THING MYSELF?
DON'T CHANGE ANY OF THE SETTINGS! TRUST THE MACHINE TO DO ITS JOB!
HEY--
WHY'S IT GOIN' NUTS? I DIDN'T TOUCH IT--I SWEAR!
RELAX! IT'S IN AUTO-AVOIDANCE MODE.
IT PICKED UP SOMEONE NEARBY AND MARCHED US TO SAFETY.
SO IT KNEW THIS CAVE WAS RIGHT HERE?
COMPUTERS KNOW EVERYTHING.
EXCEPT MAYBE WHICH MONSTER IS THE COOLEST.
SEE? WE AVOIDED AN UNNECESSARY RUN-IN WITH A FIRE TRUCK.
SYSTEM WORKED PERFECT.
YEAH. SOME FIRE TRUCK.

SO WE GONNA CAMP FOR THE NIGHT?
YEAH. THE *MULE'S* WELL-STOCKED. WE SHOULD BE PRETTY COMFORTABLE.
AN ARMY TRAVELS ON ITS STOMACH! I THINK DON DA-DOING-DOING SAID THAT.
SO LEMME ASK YA. WHAT'S WITH YOU YOUNG GUYS AND THE MILITARY?
I MEAN, WHAT'S THE ATTRACTION?
THEY FIGURED OUT HOW TO PACKAGE THE ULTIMATE HIGH, MAN.
YEAH, MY WIFE SAYS SHE LIKES IT FOR THE ADRENALINE BUZZ.
ME, I HAVE A HARD TIME GETTIN' MY HEAD AROUND THE IDEA OF TAKING ORDERS AND BEIN' SHOT AT.
MOST CIVILIANS DO. ESPECIALLY *OLDER* CIVILIANS.
YEAH! YOU GEN-X-Y-Z-ERS AND YOUR GEEZER PARENTS WERE THE ONES WHO LEFT ALL THESE GLOBAL CATASTROPHES.
FUCKED-UP WARS. FUCKED-UP ECONOMY. FUCKED-UP ENVIRONMENT. ALL OF IT LEFT FOR *US* TO FIX.
WHY DO Y'THINK THEY CALL US *GENERATION PWNED?*
WE'RE STUCK WITH THE JOB OF CLEANING UP YOUR DIRTY DIDEES, AT LEAST LET US HAVE A GOOD TIME DOING IT.
PULL UP A CHAIR. WE'RE GOING TO WATCH SOME SLASHER MOVIES.
THAT'S OKAY. I'M COOL.
NO! EEEEEE! HAK! CHOP!
YOU GUYS ENJOY YOURSELVES.

DIDN'T YOU GET ANY SLEEP LAST NIGHT?

AFTER *BLOOD CRACK* WE HAD TO CHECK OUT THE SEQUELS.

WITH THE *EXO-SUITS* ON AUTOMATIC, WE CAN CATCH UP ON SLEEP DURING THE MARCH.

FUCK THIS BRAINWASHED SHIT.

LET'S SEE WHAT HAPPENS IF I OPEN UP A MENU AND CLICK A FEW ITEMS...

AUTOMATIC MODE
MANUAL MODE

HEY YA, *GENERATION PWNED!* US OLD FARTS AT LEAST KNOW HOW TO RUN OUR OWN LIVES!

WHAT THE FUCK?

THE SON OF A BITCH HAS GOT IT IN *MANUAL MODE!* HE'S ENDANGERING THE MISSION!

LOMAN! SWITCH IT BACK TO AUTOMATIC-- *NOW!*

OKAY. OKAY. I WAS JUST HAVIN' A LITTLE...

HUH?

NORMAL SPEED
HIGH SPEED

BOOP

WOH! HELP! HEEELLLP!

OH, MAN. NOW THE HOSER'S KICKED THE DAMN THING INTO *HIGH SPEED!*

I TOLJA. I DON'T LIKE THIS GUY!

I GOTTA OWCH!
GET THIS THING BACK IN OOOF!
NORMAL MODE.
EEEEEEEEK!
HEY! WHAT ARE YA DOIN'?
I CAN'T STEER IF I CAN'T SEE!
GET OFFA ME, YOU LITTLE-- AAUGH!
EEEEEK!
BLANG
EEEEEEEEK!
BLONG
KLANG
WHANG
DONG

AIR BAGS, MAN.
REALLY GREAT TECHNOLOGY.

NOT MUCH PROTECTION AGAINST YOU GETTING YOUR HEAD SHOT CLEAN--

TWO DOWN!
THREE
GO IN THE TRUCK!
BRRIIIP
ROYDEN DRIFTS BACK WITH THE CLAYMORE MINE AND...
PUNT
HE SCORES!

SYNCHRONIZE AND LIFT...
HOOF!
I FEEL LIKE A TOTAL SPAZ. I ALMOST GOT US ALL KILLED.
WORSE, MAN. YOU COULD HAVE HURT MY MAGIC MONKEY, TOO.
AUTO-REBOOT
SHE'S REBOOTING. WE'RE GOOD TO GO.
I LEARNED MY LESSON. FROM NOW ON I'LL LET THE MACHINE DO ITS JOB.
HEY, MAGICIAN.
I THINK IT'S TIME YOU AND I LEVELED WITH EACH OTHER.
HOW SO?
I KNOW ABOUT THE RETREATS. HOW THEY'RE AS MUCH AN ATTRACTION AS COMBAT FOR YOU GUYS.
AND I ALSO KNOW WHAT'S GOIN' ON WITH YOU AND THE WIFE.
I WASN'T GONNA SAY ANYTHING, BUT SEEING HOW YOU SAVED MY KAZOO BACK THERE...
SHE AND I GOT AN UNDERSTANDING. KNOW WHAT I'M SAYIN'?
YEAH. I THINK I DO.
YOU GUYS READY TO MAKE LIKE ROA RUNNERS?
BEEP BEEP!
BEEP BEEP!

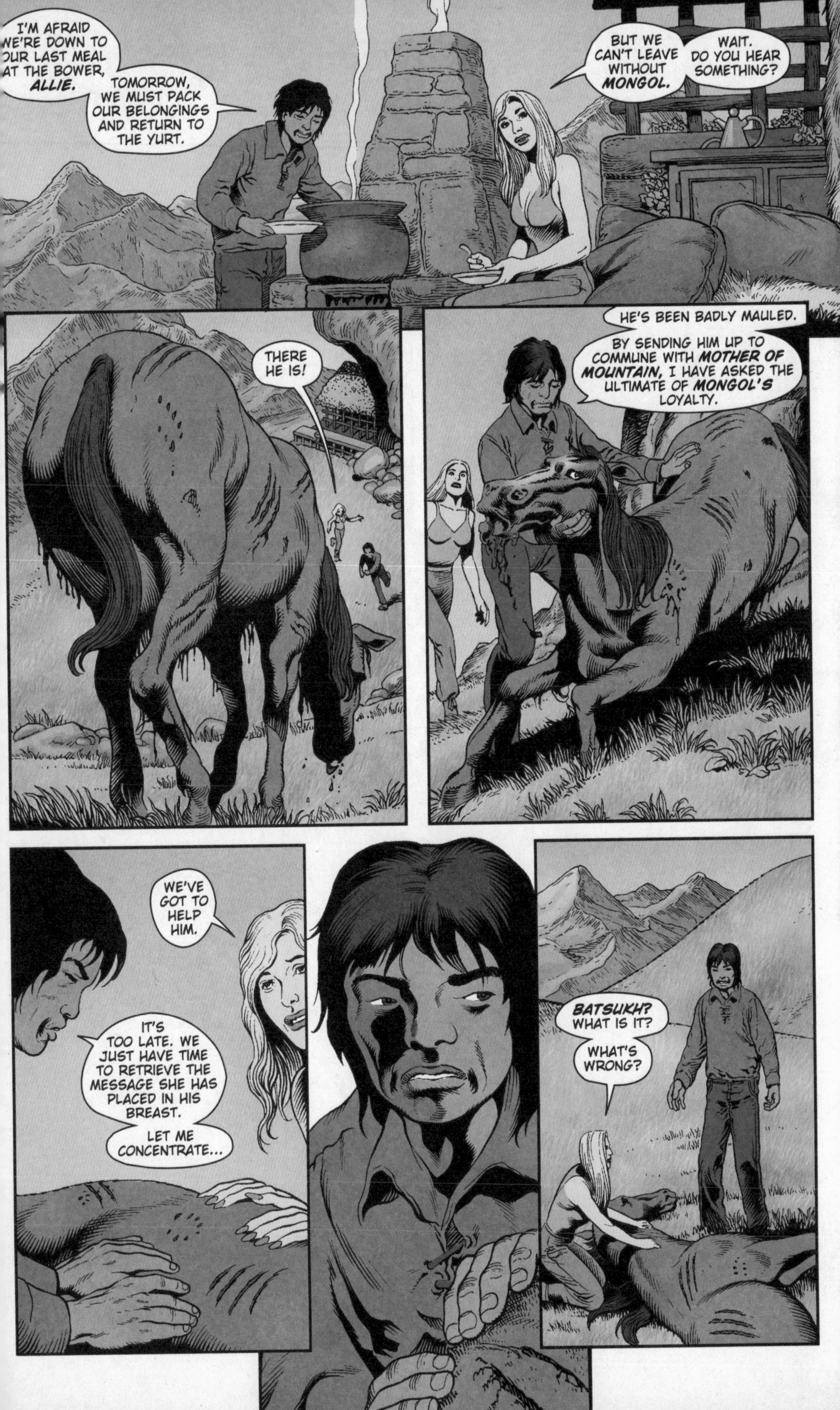
I'M AFRAID WE'RE DOWN TO OUR LAST MEAL AT THE BOWER, ALLIE.
TOMORROW, WE MUST PACK OUR BELONGINGS AND RETURN TO THE YURT.
BUT WE CAN'T LEAVE WITHOUT MONGOL.
WAIT. DO YOU HEAR SOMETHING?
THERE HE IS!
HE'S BEEN BADLY MAULED.
BY SENDING HIM UP TO COMMUNE WITH MOTHER OF MOUNTAIN, I HAVE ASKED THE ULTIMATE OF MONGOL'S LOYALTY.
WE'VE GOT TO HELP HIM.
IT'S TOO LATE. WE JUST HAVE TIME TO RETRIEVE THE MESSAGE SHE HAS PLACED IN HIS BREAST.
LET ME CONCENTRATE...
BATSUKH? WHAT IS IT?
WHAT'S WRONG?

THE MOTHER SHOWED ME OUR FUTURE.
I SAW *YOU.* BUT YOU WERE ENRAGED. SPITTING IN MY FACE. CLAWING MY EYES.
TH-THEN TURNING AWAY LIKE A WOMAN SCORNED.
THEN *MOTHER OF MOUNTAIN* IS WRONG, *BATSUKH.*

I'M NOT LEAVING YOU. EVER!
I DON'T WANT TO BE THE SAD AND HOPELESS *ALLIE* WHO LIVED IN THE MACHINE WORLD ANYMORE.
I ONLY WANT TO BE THE PERSON I SEE REFLECTED IN *YOUR* EYES.

IT'S NOT THAT SIMPLE, *ALLIE.*

YOU HAVE THE GIFT.
SEE FOR YOURSELF BEFORE POOR MONGOL BREATHES HIS LAST.
OKAY. LET ME JUST CALM MYSELF AND....

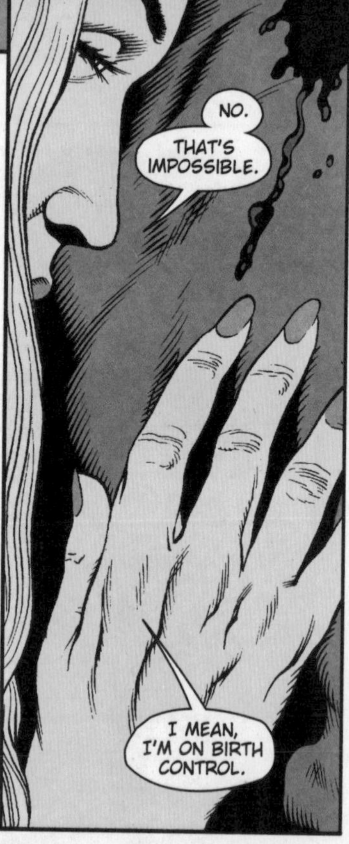
NO.
THAT'S IMPOSSIBLE.
I MEAN, I'M ON BIRTH CONTROL.

I *CAN'T* BE PREGNANT!

FORWARD OPERATING BASE HABITRAIL. BABEL PROVINCE, AFBAGHISTAN
WELLLL... SHOULD I?
KNOCK KNOCK
HULLO. SWITZER? YOU HOME?
A FEW YEARS FROM NOW.
YO, BEAU! DID YOU ASK YOUR PHONE HONEY OUT YET?
AWWW, I'M TOO SCARED.
THIS WILL PUT SOME LEAD IN YOUR PENCIL.
IT'S A NEW FLAVOR: CHOCO-LIPSYNC.
BUT I NEVER BEEN ON A DATE BEFORE.
NO GIRL AS NICE AS POOKIE WOULD EVER GO OUT WITH ME.
BUT WE SENT HER THAT PHOTO OF FLABBERGAST, REMEMBER?
I GUARANTEE SHE'LL PICK UP ON THE FIRST RING.
Siigh OKAY.
WISH ME LUCK.
bu beep beep boop
HELLO?
HI, POOKIE. IT'S ME, BEAU.
HOW YA DOING?
OH, I'M... REALLY WELL, BEAU. A-AND I'M JUST...SO HAPPY TO HEAR A FRIENDLY VOICE.

I'VE BEEN SITTING HERE STARING AT YOUR PICTURE, JUST HOPING YOU'D CALL.
I WAS WONDERIN' IF, YOU KNOW, YOU MIGHT BE FREE TOMORROW NIGHT?
MAYBE WE COULD WATCH TANTRATUBBIES TOGETHER?
THERE'S SO MUCH I WANT TO KNOW ABOUT YOU!
CONNECTIONS I'D LOVE TO MAKE.
OH, YES! THAT WOULD BE WONDERFUL!
The Amazing Flabbergast
Support our Troops at CASINO NIGHT
Sponsored by the STELAPHANE FOUNDATION
Support our T
CASINO N
Sponsored by
STELAPHANE FOU
U.S. SECRETARY OF WAR STELAPHANE
I'LL BE COUNTING THE MINUTES UNTIL TOMORROW NIGHT!
OKAY. 'BYE.
HA! YOU DOG, YOU!
LISTEN, I GOTTA CATCH MY PLANE. FEEL FREE TO USE MY DIGS WHILE I'M IN EDGEFIELD.
JUST DON'T DO ANYTHING I WOULDN'T DO.
OKAY.
THANKS FOR HELPIN' ME, SWITZER.
NO SWEAT.
I ONLY WISH MY OWN PROBLEMS WITH THE OPPOSITE SEX WERE AS EASY TO SOLVE!

SILK ROAD, UPPER MONGROLIA
HEY, DON'T THESE THINGS EVER NEED GAS?
MOST OF THE NEW STUFF IS NUKE-POWERED THESE DAYS.
RUNS FOREVER. CIVILIANS AREN'T SUPPOSED TO KNOW, THOUGH.
WHEW! EVEN WITH THAT FUCKED-UP FIREFIGHT YESTERDAY, WE'VE MADE OVER A THOUSAND MILES.
WHY DON'T WE CAMP FOR THE NIGHT?
YEAH, MY ASS IS READY FOR A PIT STOP.
OKAY, LOMAN. TELL THE COMPUTER TO FIND US A GOOD SITE. JUST BE CAREFUL WHICH BUTTON YOU PUSH THIS TIME.
I HEAR YA.
LOOKY THAT! MACHINE FOUND A NICE BIG CAVE OFF THE BEATEN PATH. PERFECT SPOT.
HOW DID IT KNOW IT WAS HERE?
COMPUTERS KNOW EVERYTHING.
UH-OH. LOOKS LIKE THIS BOLT HOLE'S GOT INHABITANTS. THE KIND THAT EAT HORSES.
IF THE MACHINE'S MARCHING US IN, THEN IT MUST BE SAFE.

SOMEBODY'S LIVING IN HERE.
NOT RECENTLY. THE FIRE'S COLD.
CRYSTALS. DRIED PLANTS. I BET IT'S ONE OF THOSE CRAZY NEW AGE HERMITS YOU HEAR ABOUT.
FROM THE LOOKS OF IT, THEY'RE INTO THE SAME SORT OF WICCAN SHIT THAT HOOKED *YOU*, FLAB-DUDE.

BLOOD, BATH AND BEYOND

WHAT YOU GOT THERE, ROYDEN?
IT'S THESE HERBS DRYING OVER THE HEARTH.
THEY'RE KIND OF FAMILIAR...
IN FACT, THEY'RE RIGHT OUT OF "CHEECH AND CHONG MEET PREDATOR"!
OUR MYSTERY HERMIT IS A SERIOUS STONER!
I BET I CAN MAKE A RIGHTEOUS BONG OUT OF THE MULE'S CHEMISTRY SET.
HEY, IS THAT COL BEER IN THERE?
GUYS-- ARE YOU SURE IT'S A GOOD IDEA TO GO INTC PARTY MODE?
Kff.
AH, FUCK IT.
Wwohhhh.
I'M SERIOUSLY BAKED.
I GOTTA WATCH SOME HORROR MOVIES! HOW ABOUT YOU GUYS?
I'M FINE OUT HERE.
ME TOO.

UNREAL, HUH?
WHAT-- THE STARS? OR THE WEED?
YOU AND ME. ENDIN' UP WAY OUT HERE TOGETHER. WHAT WITH YOU DOIN' THE WIFE AND EVERYTHING.
THANKS FOR BEING SO COOL ABOUT IT.
TNK
GOT TO ADMIT I WAS A LITTLE FREAKED WHEN I CLIMBED IN THE BACK OF THE TAXI.
IT'S TOUGH BEING A GUY SOMETIMES. ESPECIALLY WHEN THERE'S THAT KIND OF REALLY TIGHT CONNECTION, Y'KNOW?
Y'MEAN THE JEALOUSY THING?
I'M NOT GONNA BULLSHIT YA, LOMAN. I'M GOB-SMACKED.
SHE THINKS IT'S A BIG JOKE, 'CAUSE I GOT TAGGED WITH THIS WICCAN LOVE CHARM.
BUT I'M NOT SO SURE THAT HAD ANYTHING TO DO WITH IT.
SO YOU REALLY STUCK ON HER?
I LOVE HER ASS TOO, MAN. BUT SHE'S GOT A TASTE FOR THE BAD BOYS.
SO WHAT ARE GUYS LIKE US GONNA DO, HUH?
MAYBE, DEEP DOWN, IT'S THE REAL REASON WHY WE DIG HER?
Y'KNOW-- A FEW MORE ≷Uuurp≶ BEERS AND I MIGHT START AGREEING WITH YOU.

SINKYANG FRONTIER, OUTER MONGROLIAN REPUBLIC
MONGOL HAD SUCH A BEAUTIFUL AURA.
I'M SO SORRY HE HAD TO DIE, BATSUKH.
IF WHAT MOTHER OF MOUNTAIN SAID IS TRUE, THEN THE HORSE IS THE LEAST OF OUR PROBLEMS.
IS IT SO TERRIBLE IF...I'M PREGNANT?
MY LIFE HAS CHANGED SO MUCH SINCE I'VE MET YOU. I FEEL LIKE A NEW PERSON.
I NEVER WANTED A CHILD BEFORE, BUT NOW... I'M READY. I KNOW I AM.
OH, ALLIE. IT WASN'T SUPPOSED TO HAPPEN LIKE THIS.
I'VE DONE THINGS. SOME AWFUL THINGS.
HUSH.
I DON'T CARE WHAT HAPPENED IN THE PAST. WE NEED TO FOCUS ON OUR BABY'S FUTURE.
WE'VE CREATED A NEW LIFE, BATSUKH. THROUGH OUR LOVE.
WHAT COULD POSSIBLY BE WRONG WITH THAT?

IT IS THE SECOND PART OF MOTHER'S PROPHECY THAT I FEAR.
SHE SAID YOU WOULD TURN ON ME AND FLEE BACK TO THE MACHINE WORLD.
LET'S JUST SAY "TO HELL WITH MOTHER'S PROPHECY." CAN'T WE STAY UP HERE IN OUR BOWER...
BONNG GOONNG
...FOREVER?
BLEAAAGHHH! YAH! YAH!
APPARENTLY WE CAN'T, ALLIE...
BLAAUUOOW! BLAAUUOOW!
RREEEAAAAWWWH!
THE MOTHER HAS CAST US OUT...

Afbaghistan International Airport
Yeah, I'm just connecting with him now. Don't know what condition he'll be in.
I'll give the Colonel your regards, Secretary Stelaphane. 'Bye!
Motivation and Morale
Hello, Colonel Healey! I'm back.
What's this I hear about our wannabe rock star landing in the hospital?
Did he plug his guitar into the wrong...?
Uh... you okay, Colonel?
I'm fine.
You look a little stressed. I brought the book, maybe we should try a new position?
No.
I want Allie.
But I can't have her.
And it's all your fault.
Babylon General Hospital
Admitting
VIP
Sir, what do you mean? You signed off on sending her away.
Motivation and Morale
Maybe. But I wasn't given complete information.
I know what's going on. You and Stelaphane are in cahoots.
Visiting
H-have you been taking your medications, sir?
Once Magoon gets released, he'll be handling my meds, Lieutenant.

SO DEE DEE GEST PUT ME IN TOUCH WITH A DESIGNER-SURGEON WHO RECONSTRUCTED EVERYTHING.
HE USED A HUMAN-HYBRIDIZED STEM CELL CULTURE FROM A KENTUCKY DERBY WINNER. IF IT TAKES, I CAN ALWAYS GET A JOB DOING PORN VIDEOS.
BE SURE TO FOLLOW THE DOCTOR'S ORDERS. WE ALL KNOW WHAT HAPPENS TO Ahem PEOPLE WHO FALL OFF THEIR MEDS.
Hmmmf.
I NEVER SHOULD HAVE FUCKED AROUND WITH THOSE EXTADRINES. I WAS SO OUT OF IT, I DUNNO WHO EVEN ASSAULTED ME.
THE MILITARY POLICE SAID WITH THE SUPER-GLUE, THE GUITAR AND THE BUZZ-JOB THEY FIGURE IT MUST HAVE BEEN COLLEGE KIDS.
NO KIDDING? GEE, THAT'S TERRIBLE.
SO SHALL WE START OUR MEETING THEN...?
WHAT ABOUT THIS DRUG YOU TOOK?
IT'S AN ADVANCE PROGRAMMING PSYCHEDELIC. COMES IN A WI-FI CAPSULE THAT MAPS THE USER RIGHT INTO BIG FINGER'S QUANTUM CORE.
BEING IN THERE IS LIKE SWIMMING IN THE MIND OF GOD. OR MAYBE THE DEVIL. IT'S HARD TO TELL.
IT TAUGHT ME A TUNE, SIR. QUITE DELIBERATELY, IN FACT.
I'LL PLAY YOU A DEMO I MADE...
UMM, THANKS, BUT WE'VE GOT A LOT TO GO OVER...
I WANT TO HEAR IT.

IT'S REAL SIMPLE. IT GOES LIKE THIS...
GIMME GIMME, OOH OOH. GIMME GIMME, OOH AH.
Siigh
MM-HMM. MM-HMM.

GIMME GIMME, OOH OOH. GIMME GIMME, OOH AH.
UH-HUH. UH-HUH!
GEE. IT IS KIND OF CATCHY.

GIMME GIMME, OOH OOH. GIMME GIMME, OOH AH.
TO ME IT'S LIKE... A GIFT. I THINK I MAY GIVE UP THIS WHOLE FANTASY OF BEING A ROCK STAR AND MAYBE DEVOTE MYSELF TO CONTEMPLATION.
THAT'S NICE. BUT WE REALLY HAVE TO GET ON TO THE DETAILS OF THE NEXT RETREAT. SECRETARY STELAPHANE HAD A FEW SUGGESTIONS THAT--
NO, WAIT. WAIT!
LISTEN TO THIS THING! IT'S RETRO AND TECHNO AND DISCO AND...

GIMME GIMME, OOH OOH. GIMME GIMME, OOH AH.
SEXY! JESUS, IT'S IRRESISTIBLE.
AND THE LYRICS ARE JUST SO NOW!
ARE YOU HEARING SOMETHING I'M MISSING, SIR, BECAUSE...?

I'M WALLOWING IN IT.
RUBBING MY WHOLE BODY UP AGAINST A GREAT...BIG... FAT...
HIT.

THENNNNNNN...RELEASE THE SINGLE!
WHAT DO YOU SAY, MAGOON? YOU READY TO GET UP THERE AND KNOCK "LITTLE SPEED BOAT" OFF ITS THRONE?
OKAY! WE SLIP IT IN BEHIND THE NEXT BRACE OF RECRUITING ADS. MAKE IT THE SUBLIMINAL THEME SONG OF THE WHOLE HOT ZONE CLUB CAMPAIGN!
PLANT IT LIKE A WASP EGG IN THE MINDS OF EVERY 12-TO 24-YEAR-OLD WITH AN INTERNET CONNECTION.
YOU MEAN, YOU WANT ME TO PERFORM? LIKE, IN CONCERTS AND VIDEOS?
WHO ELSE? YOU'RE THE ARTIST WHO RISKED MANHOOD AND SANITY TO BRING US THIS CULTURAL TREASURE!
I THINK WE'LL KEEP THE HAIR JUST LIKE IT IS. IT'S TOTALLY TELEPATHIC.
ARE YOU GETTING THIS DOWN, LIEUTENANT?
YES, SIR. BUT ARE YOU SURE THIS IS A GOOD USE OF MOMO'S TIME AND...?
IT'S GOING TO DRIVE RECRUITMENT THROUGH THE STRATOSPHERE.
SO MAYBE WE'RE NOT CURING CANCER. BUT MAGOON HAS GIVEN US SOMETHING THIS TROUBLED OLD WORLD SORELY NEEDS...
A MONSTER RING TONE.
AND WE'LL BE SETTIN' OUT FOR HEAVEN IN MY LITTLE SPEED BOAT!

DEE DEE GEST.
HI, POMONA. LISTEN, GIRLFRIEND, CAN I CALL YOU BACK? I'M NOT AT MY DESK RIGHT NOW AND...
YOU'RE WHERE?
I'M DOWN IN EMERGENCY! WE CAME RIGHT FROM THE BEACH!
THE DOCTOR SAYS THERE'S NOTHING HE CAN DO FOR ME!
CALM DOWN! WHAT HAPPENED? ARE YOU HURT?
STELAPHANE TURNED HIS AWFUL ACTIVE DENIAL SYSTEM ON ME. THE MICROWAVES DID SOMETHING TO MY BUTT IMPLANTS.
NOW MY ASS LOOKS LIKE MUTATED MAC AND CHEESE!
EVERY MAN IN THE LOBBY EXCEPT FOR ISSA IS LAUGHING AT ME! EVEN THE DOCTOR COULDN'T HOLD BACK WHEN HE SAW IT!
HE FINALLY GAVE UP AND SENT ME HOME!
I NEED A REPAIR SPECIALIST, DEE DEE, AND I NEED ONE NOW!
A SURGICAL SKILL SET FOR SILICON FAILURE IS VERY HIGH END. IT'S GOING TO BE BIG MONEY.
BUT I'M BROKE AND DADDY'S CUT ME OFF.
OH GOD, I'M PROBABLY UP ON YOUTUBE ALREADY!
IT'S GOING TO TAKE ME TIME TO LINE UP THE RIGHT GUY FOR THIS, POMONA.
HAVE ISSA BRING YOU HOME, THEN CALL IN SICK AT THE DEALERSHIP UNTIL YOU HEAR FROM ME. AND BE READY TO WRITE A SEVEN-FIGURE CHECK.
BUT WITH MY BOOTY LOOKIN LIKE THIS I CAN'T SELL CARS!

THEY'RE ALL HOWLING AT ME! MAKE IT STOP, ISSA! PLEASE!
I HAVE AN IDEA, MISS POMONA.
STAY BEHIND ME. WE'LL SLIP INTO THIS LAUNDRY ROOM...
Laundry
I'LL NEVER MAKE ANOTHER SALE WITH A BUTT FULL OF SAGGING SILLY PUTTY! I MIGHT AS WELL KILL MYSELF BEFORE I STARVE TO DEATH!
LET'S JUST GET YOU HOME, MA'AM. HERE--PUT ON THIS FULL BODY BURKHA.
YOU'LL NEED TO LEAVE SOME MONEY TO RECOMPENSE THE RIGHTFUL OWNER.
THIS IS WHAT IT'S COME TO.
AN ASS SO PREPOSTEROUS I'VE GOT TO BE WRAPPED IN A CIRCUS TENT TO GET ACROSS THE LOBBY.
THE BURKHA IS ACTUALLY A VERY SENSIBLE GARMENT. YOU MIGHT FIND THE EXPERIENCE OF WEARING ONE... ENLIGHTENING.
THAT'S ODD. THOSE SAME GOOFBALLS WHO WERE OUT MOCKING ME EARLIER TOOK ONE LOOK AT THE BURKHA AND AVERTED THEIR EYES.
IT SENDS A SIMPLE MESSAGE THAT EVEN LOUTS UNDERSTAND.
EVERY MAN WE PASS JUST LOOKS DOWN AND NODS. WHAT'S GOING ON?
IN MY CULTURE, WHEN A WOMAN WEARS A BURKHA IT IS PERCEIVED AS A SIGN OF RESPECT. ONE THAT MEN AUTOMATICALLY RETURN.
YES, BUT ISN'T FORCING WOMEN TO COVER THEIR BODIES A WAY OF HOLDING US BACK?
THE BURKHA IS A PRACTICAL ANSWER TO AN UNDENIABLE FACT. A WOMAN'S GOD-GIVEN SEXUALITY IS TOO OVER-POWERING TO INCORPORATE INTO EVERYDAY COMMUNITY.
AND COMMERCE.

MECCAWAY MALL
I'VE NEVER EXPERIENCED THAT KIND OF RESPONSE FROM MEN BEFORE. IT WAS KIND OF... DISORIENTING.
LET'S STOP HERE AND STROLL AROUND SOME MORE. YOU NEED SOME NEW CLOTHES, DON'T YOU?
YES! THANK YOU, MISS POMONA.
WHY DO THE OTHER WOMEN IN BURKHAS WALK A FEW STEPS BEHIND THEIR HUSBANDS?
WELL, IN ZEROMOSTELIANISM, IT IS SEEN AS RECOGNITION THAT ALL MEN ARE MANIFESTATIONS OF THE MASCULINE SIDE OF GOD.
MEN RETURN THE FAVOR, BOWING BEFORE THE ETERNAL FEMININE.
MOST MODERN CONSUMER CULTURE HIGHLIGHTS SEXUALITY BUT IGNORES THE SPIRITUAL. AND THAT LEADS TO ALL SORTS OF DEVIANT THINKING.
YES. I SEE.
OR AT LEAST I...I THINK I'M BEGINNING TO.
50% OFF!
THANK YOU FOR LETTING ME PICK OUT MORE SENSIBLE CLOTHING, MISS POMONA. IT MEANS A LOT TO ME.
CLOTHING CAN CERTAINLY AFFECT ONE'S EXPERIENCE. I JUST BOUGHT THREE MORE BURKHAS.
AND PLEASE, DROP THE MISS AND MA'AM. JUST CALL ME POMONA FROM NOW ON.
HOW ABOUT YOU TAKING THE WHEEL FOR THE DRIVE HOME?
WHY, YES, MISS...I MEAN, POMONA.
I'D BE HONORED.

H-HAVE I BROUGHT SOME SORT OF CURSE DOWN ON US, BATSUKH?
NONE OF THIS IS YOUR FAULT, ALLIE.
WE'LL BE AT THE YURT SHORTLY.
I'M SURE WE'LL FIND A WARM WELCOME...
THAT'S ODD. NO ONE TO GREET US?
嘿你婦女 帶來毯子
你新的姐妹來了
她在地獄可以燒!
THOSE ARE MY THINGS! WHY ARE THEY THROWING THEM OUT?
什麼是你瘋狂婦女做?
PATOOEY!
我們不讓那個巫婆進來這裡
BOSS--WE GOT PROBLEMS!

ONE OF THE WIVES WAS NOSING AROUND IN ALLIE'S TORN PARKA AND FOUND THIS MAGIC CHARM!
NOW THEY'RE ALL CONVINCED SHE'S A WITCH AND HAS YOU UNDER HER SPELL.
TELL THEM I DON'T KNOW ANYTHING ABOUT IT!
WHATEVER THE THING IS MUST HAVE BEEN PLANTED IN MY FLIGHT SUIT BY THE PEOPLE WHO DRUGGED AND DROPPED ME HERE.
TELL THEM I'M NOT A WITCH, BATSUKH. I'M JUST A WOMAN. ONE WHO'S EXPECTING YOUR CHILD.
TELL THEM I WANT NOTHING MORE THAN TO GIVE BIRTH IN THE YURT AND BRING THE BABY UP ALONG WITH ITS BROTHERS AND SISTERS.
IT'S TOO LATE TO REASON WITH THEM. THIS IS WHAT THE MOTHER WAS WARNING US OF...
THERE'S ANOTHER PROBLEM, BOSS. THE MINISTER OF CULTURE WAS HERE WHILE YOU WERE GONE. HE WANTS ANOTHER QUARTER MILLION FOR THE PERMITS.
THERE'S NO WAY WE CAN RAISE THAT KIND OF MONEY. THE GREEDY LITTLE SHIT'S BLEEDING ME WHITE!
THEN WE'RE BASICALLY FUCKED.
WH-WHAT IS SHE TALKING ABOUT, BATSUKH?
I THOUGHT BREE WAS ONE OF YOUR WIVES. WHY IS SHE CALLING YOU "BOSS"?
I WAS GOING TO TELL YOU, ALLIE.
I SWEAR.

DEEP DOWN I AM A MAN OF TRUTH. MY WIVES. MY CHILDREN. MY PEOPLE. I LOVE THEM ALL.
I THOUGHT I COULD SAVE THEIR CULTURE. STOP THIS WHOLE WAY OF LIFE FROM DISAPPEARING.
B-BUT I GOT IN OVER MY HEAD. AND THEN YOU CAME INTO MY LIFE...
OH, I WISH TO GOD I'D NEVER HEARD ABOUT MOTHER OF MOUNTAIN! NEVER SIGNED ON TO THIS CRAZY IDEA!
COME DOWN FROM YOUR MOUNTAIN, BITCH!
COME PICK CLEAN THIS BROKEN, EMPTY HUSK THAT ONCE WAS BATSUKH'S SOUL!
WHAT'S THAT?
Bzzorrrk!
IT IS HER.
I DON'T KNOW.
IT SOUNDS MORE LIKE SOMEONE...
Zznnnnfff!
Snnnzzzz!
...SNORING.

AND YOU KNOW WHAT? I'VE HEARD THAT SNORE SOMEWHERE BEFORE!
LOMAN! IS THAT YOU?
HUH? OH, YEAH. HOWZIT GOIN'?
BLEEUUUGHH!
MOUTH TASTES LIKE THE INSIDE OF AHAB'S UNDERPANTS.
PARTIED HEARTY LAS NIGHT.
MUST HAVE POLISHED OFF THE WHOLE CAS BETWEEN US.
Snnnoooorrrk!
NOT TO MENTION A HALF OUNCE OF SKUNK. OOOOG.
HERE COME MY BUDDIES NOW. DON'T WAKE 'EM UP.
LOMAN, WHAT ARE YOU DOING WAY OUT HERE? WHAT'S GOING ON?
WELL, UMMM... YOU GOT SHANGHAIED, RIGHT?
I'M HERE TO TAKE YOU HOME.
GRAB YOUR STUFF.

NEWARK INTERNATIONAL AIRPORT.
OH, HI, BEAU. YEAH, WE'RE JUST LANDING NOW.
I'M STILL CONFUSED. LIKE I HAVE TO MAKE SOME SORT OF CHOICE, Y'KNOW?
BA 35L R
BUT I'M LOOKING FORWARD TO HAVING SOME TIME TO MULL THINGS OVER BEFORE LOMAN GETS BACK.
HOW ABOUT YOU? ANY PRE-DATE BUTTERFLIES YET?
I'M TINGLING ALL OVER, SWITZER.
JUST DON'T TELL MY MOM, OKAY? I DON'T THINK SHE COULD HANDLE ME DATING YET.
ARE YOU KIDDING? ONCE DEE DEE HEARS ABOUT POOKIE SHE'LL BE PLANNING THE WEDDING!
THERE'S MY DAD. LISTEN, CALL ME AFTER. I WANT A FULL REPORT.
I'LL SEE YOU BACK IN THE SANDBOX IN A COUPLE WEEKS. 'BYE!
HIYA, SKABIBBLE!
IT'S SUCH A RELIEF TO SEE YOU SAFE AND SOUND. YOUR MOTHER AND I PRAY EVERY DAY...
I TOLD YOU, DADDY. I HAVE A DESK JOB.
WHERE I'M STATIONED IS SAFER THAN DOWNTOWN NEWARK.

SO THEY TELL US WE'RE MAKING PROGRESS IN THE WAR.
HOW'S WITH YOU GUYS?
WELL, THE BUILDING FUND HAS BEEN ACCRUING NICELY. I HAVE TO THANK THAT HUSBAND OF YOURS FOR PLACING SOME OF THE BEST RETURNING INVESTMENTS.
EVERYTHING OKAY WITH YOU AND LOMAN?
OH YEAH! HE JUST PAID ME THAT SURPRISE VISIT IN THE BAGH, AND WE HAD A BLAST.
AND WHAT'S THIS?
NEW CABINETS? AND TILE? WHY DIDN'T THE BUM TELL ME?
HE WANTED IT TO BE A SURPRISE.
EVEN NEW APPLIANCES! AND THE OLD STOVE WORKED PERFECT.
HE MUST HAVE MADE A BUNCH OF MONEY IN ONE OF HIS DEALS, I BET.
LISTEN, SKABIBBLE. SOME OF LOMAN'S BUSINESS ASSOCIATES ARE A LITTLE...SHADY. KNOW WHAT I MEAN?
THIS TRIP HOME I WANT YOU TO BE EXTRA CAREFUL.
YEEEEESSSS, DADDY.
IF YOU SEE ANY BAD GUYS OUT THERE, SEND THEM AROUND SO I CAN TRY OUT MY RANGER TRAINING ON THEM.
YOUR MOTHER WORRIES. JUST BE ALERT, OKAY?
SEE YOU TOMORROW, SKABIBBLE.

OOOOH YEAAHHHHH....
NOW. WHERE WAS I?
LAAADIES AND GENTLEMEN...
TONIGHT, FROM THE WILD, UNTAMED COMBAT ZONES OF ANCIENT AFBAGHISTAN, WE PRESENT...
FOR YOUR ENTERTAINMENT PLEASURE...
HEH.
I CAN GO FOR SOME OF THAT RIGHT NOW.
HOW ABOUT YOU, NEEDHAWK?
PLEASHHRR. YESHHH...

SINKYANG FRONTIER, OUTER MONGROLIAN REPUBLIC
我們從未將忍耐那條母狗!
RISE AND SHINE, BOYS.
HOW YOU LIKE YOUR COFFEE?
A FEW YEARS FROM NOW.
OOOH, MY HEAD...
WHAT'S ALL THE YELLING?
FAMILY SQUABBLE.
Ssuuup THAT BLONDE WRAPPED IN THE BLANKET--HAVEN'T I SEEN HER BACK IN EDGEFIELD?
HEALEY'S WIFE. IT'S A LONG STORY.
SO, ALLIE...YOU GOT ANY CLOTHES OR ANYTHING? WE NEED TO GET THINGS MOVIN'.
I DON'T KNOW WHAT GAME YOU'RE PLAYING THIS TIME, LOMAN.
BUT I'M NOT GOING ANYWHERE.
我們恨那個巫婆!
I'M WITH BATSUKH NOW. GO AHEAD. LAUGH.
BUT HE'S A REAL MAN--HONEST AND CARING. NOT LIKE THE PYGMIES I'VE BEEN STUCK WITH IN MY LIFE.
YEAH, WELL... THIS LITTLE PYGMY'S GOT SOME ROAST BEEF FOR YA.
DEE DEE SAYS YOUR NEW SOUL MATE HERE IS WORKING UNDER-THE-TABLE FOR YOUR HUSBAND'S EX-COMPANY.
THAT'S A TOTAL LIE! TELL HIM, BATSUKH.
UH, WELL... THERE IS SOME SLIGHT TRUTH TO WHAT HE SAYS.
HEH.

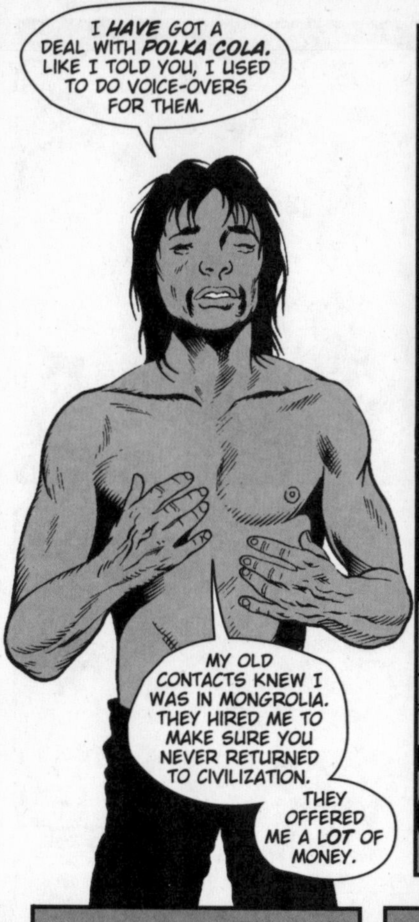
I HAVE GOT A DEAL WITH POLKA COLA. LIKE I TOLD YOU, I USED TO DO VOICE-OVERS FOR THEM.
MY OLD CONTACTS KNEW I WAS IN MONGROLIA. THEY HIRED ME TO MAKE SURE YOU NEVER RETURNED TO CIVILIZATION.
THEY OFFERED ME A LOT OF MONEY.

SEE, I'M MAKING A MOVIE. THE FOOTAGE WE'VE GOT WITH MOTHER OF MOUNTAIN IS SENSATIONAL!
THIS ISN'T JUST ANOTHER FILM, ALLIE. IT'S TAKEN OVER MY LIFE!
BUT PRODUCTION'S BEEN A NIGHTMARE. IN FAC
W-WE ALREADY LOST
ONE OF THE CAST IN
FREAK ACCIDENT.
AND NOW THE GOVERNMENT HAS DOUBLED THE FEE FOR SHOOTING PERMITS.
I'VE LOST EVERYTHING.

I-I'VE BEEN ACTING ALL ALONG, ALLIE.
LIVING AS THE CHARACTER I HOPED TO PORTRAY IN MY FILM.

I WAS HOPING TO GET AN OSCAR NOD.

THE BATSUKH I FELL IN LOVE WITH IS JUST A FUCKING FICTION!?
AGH! PLEASE, ALLIE--

LOOK AT HER GO!
SHE'S A WILDCAT!
IT'S LIKE THE JERRY SPROINGER SHOW. ALL WE NEED'S THE HOWLING AUDIENCE!
Eeeek! Eeeep!

YARHARHARHARHARHAR!
GENERATION PWNED
WHAT THE HELL'S THAT? SOME KIND OF ANIMAL?
IT'S MOVING UP THERE ON THE LEDGE.
AND IT'S BIG.
SHE IS MOTHER OF MOUNTAIN. A WERE-CREATURE WHO FEEDS ON DREAMS.
DID WE JUST SEE A YETI?
EITHER THAT OR IT'S NATIONAL GORILLA SUIT DAY.
IT WAS A MONSTER, MAN!
A REAL FUCKING MONSTER!

LET'S GET A CLOSER LOOK, FLAB!
WE'VE GOT A MISSION SITUATION HERE, ROYDEN. WE CAN'T JUST TAKE OFF ON A WILD-GOOSE CHASE.

FLAB-- YOU KNOW ME! THAT'S MY OTHER HALF UP THERE!
IF I DON'T CHECK THIS THING OUT, I'LL DEFINITELY SUFFER, LIKE, MAJOR DEPRESSION FOR THE REST OF MY LIFE.
OH, SHIT. ALL RIGHT. YOU GO ON AHEAD. THE MULE WILL TRACK YOUR EXO-SUIT.
ONCE I WRAP THINGS UP HERE, WE'LL FOLLOW.
MWUHHAHAHA!

SO, ROYDEN-- WHAT ARE YOU GOING TO DO IF YOU CATCH HER?
I DUNNO. ASK HER ABOUT THE MEANING OF LIFE, MAYBE?

她傷了我的胳膊!
MY MOVIE! MY MOOOOVIE!
她摳出了我的眼睛!
THAT WAS INCREDIBLE, ALLIE! YOU BEEN WORKING OUT?
LET'S GO.

WE'LL BOTH HAVE TO SQUEEZE INTO THE IMPERIAL WALKER.
LEMME SEE IF I CAN GET THIS THING TO LOCK IN ON ROYDEN.
ALLIE... WITHOUT MY MOVIE, WHERE SHALL I GO? WHAT SHALL I DO?
FRANKLY, BATSUKH?
I DON'T GIVE A ROLLING SHIT.
LOMAN--YOU GOT A READING?
I'M SEEING HIS HEART RATE, OXYGEN LEVELS, BRAIN ACTIVITY. SHIT LIKE THAT.
MY MOVIE...
THE COMPUTER'S PICKED UP SOMETHING ELSE MOVING OUT THERE. SOMETHING BIG.
HE'S ALMOST ON TOP OF IT.
ROYDEN-- WHAT'S ALL THIS CHANTING I'M HEARING ON THE COM-LINK?
Kora-tanay! Kong!
Otar-vay rama--Kong!
SOUNDTRACK TO KING KONG, MAN. THAT SCENE WHERE THE NATIVES CALL HIM TO THE BARRIER?
GOT IT ON MY MEDIA PLAYER. JUST SEEMED APPROPRIATE, Y'KNOW?

DON'T DO ANYTHING TILL WE GET THERE.
ROYDEN, DO YOU COPY?
Gonnnnggg!
HRrhRRRhrrr
COOOOOO

HE'S SHUT OFF HIS AUDIO.
HE PROBABLY DOESN'T WANT US TO HEAR HIM HAVING A NERDGASM.
OH.
MY.
GOD.
Hunnnph?

EASY. I-I'M NOT GONNA HURT YA. JUST WANT TO LOOK. THAT'S ALL.
CHECK OUT THOSE HOOTERS. YOU'RE ALL WOMAN, AREN'T YA?
Grrrrrrhh
GOD-- YOU'RE BEAUTIFUL! DO UNDERSTAND ME?
HRRrrRMmm

YOU DO!
I'M PUTTING THE GUN DOWN, OKAY? I JUST WANT TO TALK.
SEE, FROM THE TIME I WAS A LITTLE KID I TOTALLY LOVED--

EEEEK!
RRREEOOOOAARRRGH!
BRIIIP
--MONSTERS?
THAT WAS ROYDEN'S M-19. I HOPE HE HASN'T GONE AND SHOT SOME FUCKING ABOMINABLE SNOWMAN.
SAYS HERE HIS EXO-SUIT JUST TOOK A MAJOR HIT.
ALL HIS BIOMETRICS ARE WINKING OUT. WHAT DOES THAT MEAN?
TESTOSTERONE 0%
HORMONE 0%
BRAIN ACTIVITY 0%
IT MEANS THE MACHINE THINKS HE'S DEAD. DON'T BELIEVE IT.
I THOUGHT YOU SAID THESE MACHINES WERE ALWAYS RIGHT.
THEY ARE. EXCEPT WHEN THEY'RE WRONG.
YOU HEAR SOMETHING?
IT'S THE MAGIC MONKEY.
WHATCHA GOT, BOY?
EEEP. EEEEEP.
EEP.
AWW SHIT!

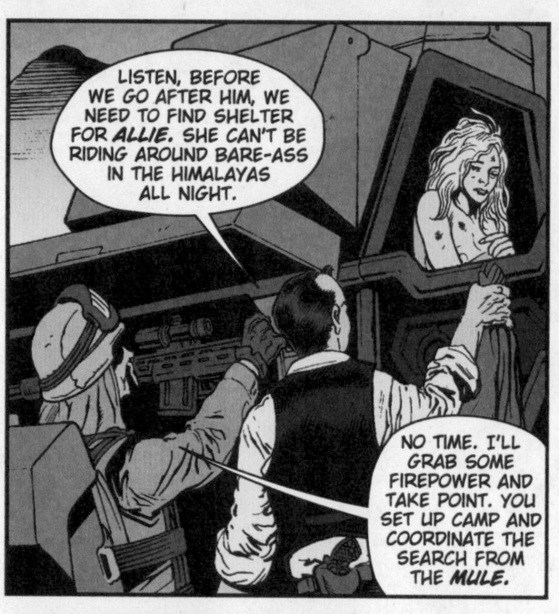
LISTEN, BEFORE WE GO AFTER HIM, WE NEED TO FIND SHELTER FOR ALLIE. SHE CAN'T BE RIDING AROUND BARE-ASS IN THE HIMALAYAS ALL NIGHT.
NO TIME. I'LL GRAB SOME FIREPOWER AND TAKE POINT. YOU SET UP CAMP AND COORDINATE THE SEARCH FROM THE MULE.

CAN DO. BUT WHAT IF ROYDEN'S HURT? WE'RE A LONG WAY FROM THE NEAREST AID STATION.
I GOT A GUY WAY UP THE LADDER WHO OWES ME A FAVOR. HE CAN PULL A STRING AND GET A MEDEVAC OUT HERE IF NEED BE.
FIRST I NEED TO FIND ROYDEN. OR WHAT'S LEFT OF HIM.

I GOTTA, TELL YA, MAN. EVERYTHING ABOUT THIS MISSION HAS TOTALLY SUCKED.
NOT EVERYTHING. I MEAN, YOU AND I GOT TO LINK UP. THAT WAS PRETTY COOL.
THE WIFE'S GONNA SHIT PERFUMED BRICKS WHEN SHE FINDS OUT I'M NEW BEST BUDS WITH HER GUY ON THE SIDE.

WELL, I GOT A FRIEND-TO-FRIEND FAVOR TO ASK, LOMAN. IF SOMETHING HAPPENS AND I DON'T MAKE IT BACK?
TELL SWITZER THAT... I WAS JUST, Y'KNOW--THINKING ABOUT HER. RIGHT UP TO THE END.
YOU GOT IT, BROTHER. BEST OF LUCK.
CATCH YOU ON THE FLIP SIDE, LOMAN.

YO, MULE. FIND US A NICE WARM CAVE TO HUNKER DOWN IN.
HOO-AH! HOO-AH!

GOT A GOOD SELECTION OF OUTERWEAR HERE. YOU STILL A 10?

I MIGHT HAVE PUT ON A LITTLE WEIGHT.

LOMAN-- WHY DID YOU COME ALL THE WAY OUT HERE FOR ME?

AHHH, I DON'T LIKE SEEING MY FRIENDS PUSHED AROUND BY ASSHOLES, Y'KNOW?

YOU WANT A HOT SHOWER?

THAT WOULD BE ***INCREDIBLE!***

I HAD THE HOOK RIGHT DOWN MY THROAT THIS TIME, LOMAN. I REALLY BELIEVED BATSUKH WAS THE ONE.
WHAT'S WRONG WITH ME? WHY AM I ATTRACTED TO NOTHING BUT ASSHOLES?

HEY, I'M A NICE GUY.
EVERY ONCE IN A WHILE THAT'S TRUE.
AND I HAVE TO ADMIT YOU'VE REALLY COME THROUGH FOR ME THIS TIME.

I WANT TO SAY "THANK YOU" BUT...AFTER ALL I'VE BEEN THROUGH, I'M NOT REALLY IN THE MOOD FOR ANYTHING. OKAY?
HEY, I'M JUST BUDDYING UP IN THE SHOWER.
THAT'S ALL.

MAN-- YOU'RE TENSE. OU HOLD IT ALL N, THAT'S YOUR PROBLEM.
LET ME USE MY LITTLE PYGMY FINGERS AND TRY TO WORK SOME OF THESE KNOTS OUT.
MMMM.
OH GOD.
YES.

LOMAN! DO YOU COPY?
THE MONKEY SEEMS TO KNOW WHERE IT'S GOING. I THINK IT'S LEADING ME BACK TO...
OH FUCK.
LOMAN! YOU THERE? I'VE FOUND ROYDEN'S EXO-SUIT. IT LOOKS LIKE A PIECE OF INSTALLATION ART.
LOMAN? DO YOU COPY?
WHAT'S GOING ON? DO THOSE OTHER TWO SOLDIERS NEED OUR HELP?
NAHH, IT'S NOTHIN'.
THEY'RE ON SOME SIMULATED TRAINING MISSION BULLSHIT.
NOTHING TO DO WITH US. I'LL SHUT IT OFF.
AUDIO OFF
SURRENDER MODE
DEACTIVATE WEAPONS
LOCATE ENEMY
I THINK I RECOGNIZED ONE OF THEM. HE'S SOME SORT OF ESCAPE ARTIST, RIGHT?
SO THEY SAY.
HEY! MY EXO-SUIT'S MARCHIN' ME AWAY!
LOMAN-- WHAT ARE YOU DOING?

NOW YOU GOT IT IN ***GOOSE-STEP MODE!***
COME ON, YOU FUCKER! WAKE UP AND RESET THE CONTROLS!
LOOOOOMAN!
WAIT A MINUTE. THIS ISN'T A ***MISTAKE,*** IS IT?
YOU'RE NOT ***REALLY*** MY BUDDY, ARE YOU?
YOU ROTTEN SON OF A BITCH.
AT LEAST ACTIVATE MY WEAPON, YOU BASTARD!
GIVE ME A FIGHTIN' CHANCE!
POINK
KLIK
KLIK
KLIK

TESTOSTERONE 0%
HORMONE 0%
BRAIN ACTIVITY 0%
FLABBERGAST
LOOKS LIKE THEY'RE GONNA HEAD STRAIGHT TO THEIR BASE.
THAT MEANS YOU AND I CAN KICK BACK HERE TONIGHT AND THEN SHOOT FOR HOME IN THE MORNING.

HOME.
I DON'T EVEN WANT TO THINK WHAT'S WAITING FOR ME THERE, ***LOMAN.***
YOU SHOULD BE THINKIN' ABOUT THE BIRD Y'GOT IN YER HAND, KIDDO. NOT THE ONES IN THE BUSH.

OUR DATA-MINE HAS STRUCK SOLID GOLD!
YOUR HANDSOME **BEAU GEST** HAS A SIDELINE AS A STAGE MAGICIAN!

ONE WHO PERFORMS AT FUNDRAISERS ORGANIZED BY THE WIFE OF THE UNITED STATES SECRETARY OF WAR!
ONE WHO WILL SOON BE OUR PUPPET, MOVING IN THE HIGHEST LEVELS OF POWER IN WASHINGTON! HAHAHA!
B-BUT, SIR. WHAT WILL HAPPEN TO **BEAU** AFTER WE...?

THAT...IS **NO...**CONCERN... OF **YOURS!**
OWW! I--I CAN'T SEE HIM **HURT,** SIR. I...OW.
SHUT UP! YOU HAVE NO FEELINGS!
AGH!
YOU HAVE ONLY **PSYCH-OP** TRAINING! AND YOU WILL USE IT TO TURN THE GRINNING FOOL INTO OUR **ZOMBIE!**

I THINK YOU NEED ANOTHER LESSON IN OBEYING ORDERS, LIEUTENANT **BOA.**
HELLO? **POOKY?** IT'S ME. **BEAU.** YOU THERE?

I WAS JUST CALLING BECAUSE IT'S TIME FOR OUR **DATE.** BUT I GUESS MAYBE YOU'RE BUSY OR SOMETHING?
ANYWAY, UM, I HOPE YOU'RE OKAY. I'LL TALK TO YOU LATER...
Click DON'T HANG UP, **BEAU!** I'M HERE!
GES

I WAS JUST... Sniff...PUTTING THE FINISHING TOUCHES ON MY...Snf... MAKE-UP.
I WAS WORRIED YOU WERE MAD AT ME.

OH NEVER, BEAU. I'M ALWAYS H-HAPPY...
Sniff JUST SO HAPPY...TO HEAR YOUR VOICE.
ME TOO. LET'S WATCH TANTRA-TUBBIES.
GEST

OOOOHHHH!
AAHHHHHH.
OMMMMMM.

WHAT DID YOU THINK, POOKY? WASN'T THAT GOOD?
OH BEAU...SOB... I CAN'T TALK TO YOU ANYMMMPH! Click

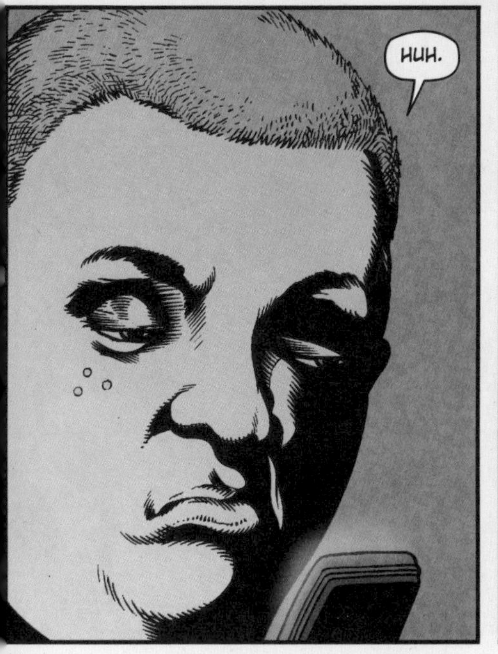
HUH.

HEY, ROY. CAN YOU TRACE A PHONE NUMBER FOR ME?
YES, CORPORAL GEST. I AM AUTHORIZED TO EAVESDROP ON ANY CIVILIAN TELECOMMUNICATIONS NETWORK OR DEVICE.

CIVILIZATION AT LAST!
HOPEFULLY WE CAN SWAP THIS TRANSFORMER FOR SOME SORT OF NORMAL RIDE.
I GOTTA KNOW, LOMAN. REALLY.
WHY DID YOU GO TO ALL THE TROUBLE OF CHASING ME DOWN?
AHHH, YOU THINK ABOUT THIS SHIT TOO MUCH.
IT'S NOT LIKE THIS MAKES US ANYTHING MORE THAN FUCK-BUDDIES.
NEVER SAID IT DID.
SWITZER AIN'T PICKING UP. I HOPE SHE'S OKAY.
GOTTA LOVE THESE REGULAR COMMUTER FLIGHTS TO NEWARK.
WAIT A MINUTE, LOMAN. OVER THERE ON THE TARMAC...
ISN'T THAT HEALEY'S MOMOMOBILE?
THE ONE WITH THE POLKA COLA AD ON THE SIDE?
HEY-- ALLIE? WHERE YOU GOIN'?
MOTIVATION AND MORALE
GIMME GIMME, OOH OOH. GIMME GIMME, OOH AH.
COME ON. THIS IS NO TIME TO ACT YOUR CRAZY BITCH SHIT. THE PLANE'S ABOUT TO LEAVE!
JUST GO.
WE HOPE YOU ENJOYED YOUR STAY IN AFBAGHISTAN, MR. LOMAN.
IT WAS FUCKIN' GREAT.

GIMME GIMME, OOH OOH. GIMME GIMME, OOH AH.
I'M HEARING PURE, UNADULTERATED SONIC CRACK, **MAGOON!** AND THE WHOLE WORLD'S GOING TO PAY **US** FOR EVERY HIT.
SIR, AS YOUR #1 ADVISOR, I THINK WE SHOULD RUN THIS NEW INITIATIVE BY SECRETARY **STELAPHANE.**

MAGOON IS MY #1 ADVISOR NOW, **WOYNER.**
HE UNDERSTANDS ME.

SIR, I DISCOVERED THIS **SURVEILLANCE** CLIP ON MAGOON'S HARD DRIVE.
HEY! WHERE'D YOU...?
ROUND AND ROUND THE MULBERRY BUSH...
ISN'T THAT YOU, **WOYNER?** AND...ME?

IS THERE NO ONE I CAN TRUST ANYMORE?
CONGRATULATIONS! YOU'VE CAUSED THE COLONEL TO HAVE ANOTHER PANIC ATTACK!
YOU SUPER-GLUED MY DICK TO MY STRAT-O-CASTER!

IS THERE **NO ONE** I CAN PUT MY FAITH IN?
SHE'S A THREAT TO EVERYTHING WE'RE PLANNING, SIR!
HE'S A BROWN-NOSING SYCOPHANT, SIR.
AHEM.

CAN I GET A WORD IN EDGEWAYS?
ALLIE?

MY GUINEVERE! YOU'VE BEEN RETURNED TO ME SAFE AND SOUND!
OH NOOOO.
STOP HEMORRHAGING BULLSHIT, HEALEY.
YOUR WORK-SLUT OVER THERE JUST HAD ME KIDNAPPED. THEN PAWNED ME OFF ON SOME DOWN-AND-OUT FILM-MAKER IN OUTER MONGROLIA.
ALL PAID FOR BY THE GOOD CORPORATE CITIZENS OF POLKA COLA! WHAT DO YOU HAVE TO SAY TO THAT?
IT'S STELAPHANE! HE PUT ME ON HIS HORRID TRUTH TEST MACHINE. HE DEMANDED MY CONTACTS IN THE FRONT OFFICE.
I KNOW I'VE NOT BEEN PAYING YOU ENOUGH ATTENTION, ALLIE. BUT I WOULD NEVER, EVER, EVER HURT YOU.
ALL I WANT IS TO MAKE OUR MARRIAGE WOR I REALLY NEE STABILITY RIGHT NOW.
RAYGUNTH
GOOD
YOU NEED STABILITY. HOW ABOUT MY NEEDS, HEALEY?
I MEANT TO SAY OUR NEEDS, ALLIE. AS A COUPLE.
MAYBE IT'S TIME TO THINK ABOUT YOU AND I STARTING A FAMILY.
WELL, I THINK IT'S TIME TO START TALKING TO THE MILITARY POLICE! KIDNAPPING IS A FELONY!
BUT I HAD NOTHING TO DO WITH IT!
I CAN VOUCH FOR THE COLONEL ON THIS, MRS. HEALEY.
YOUR ABDUCTION WAS PLANNED AND EXECUTED BY LIEUTENANT WOYNER.
TO SEE JUSTICE DONE, I'D BE WILLING TO TESTIFY UNDER OATH THAT YOUR HUSBAND WAS COMPLETELY OUT OF THE LOOP.
YOU SACK OF SHIT!

TELL YOU WHAT, HEALEY. I'M WILLING TO GIVE OUR MARRIAGE ANOTHER SHOT--FOR MY OWN REASONS.
BUT WOYNER GOES. AND WE PRESS CHARGES.
I AM IN SUCH AWE OF YOU, ALLIE.
DON'T DO THIS, SIR. YOU'RE TOO FRAGILE.
SHE'LL DESTROY YOU. SHE'LL...
GRNNNGRNNNN
SIR?
SECRETARY STELAPHANE WILL SEE YOU IN THE COLLECTION ROOM, LIEUTENANT.
WHO LET THE AIR OUT OF YOUR POTATO CHIP BAG, WOYNER?
BAD NEWS, SIR. ALLIE'S BACK.
AND SHE'S GOT COLONEL HEALEY WRAPPED AROUND HER LITTLE PINKY.
SHE JUST HAD ME FIRED. AND PLANS TO HAVE ME INDICTED FOR KIDNAPPING.
YOU'RE UNDER THE PROTECTION OF MY OFFICE NOW, WOYNER.
THIS TEMPORAL SIGNALING THING IS GETTING VERY INTERESTING. I THINK YOU AND I ARE GOING TO BE SPENDING A LOT OF TIME ON IT.
YOU'RE HIRING ME? THANK YOU, SIR! WHAT CAN I EVER DO TO...?
CHECK THIS OUT. LBJ'S GALL BLADDER.
I JUST FOUND SOME STONES TO GO WITH IT.

RADIANT LEADER IS GOING TO MAKE ME FUCKIN' RICH AFTER THIS.
HOW 'BOUT A LITTLE DRINK? WE GOTTA CELEBRATE.
NO! I WILL NEVER HURT BEAU!
HE LOVES ME-- I KNOW! AND I LOVE HIM!
HE'S MY P-PRINCE CHARMING.
WHASSAMATTER-- YOU WON'T HAVE A DRINK WITH ME?
AGHH!
I'LL SHOW YOU HOW TO DRINK!
KOF! SPUT!
FVOOOOM
OOPS. PRESSED THE WRONG BUTTON. SORRY.
I'M LOOKING FOR SOMEONE NAMED POOKY PYWACKET?

HEY, ARE YOU HURTING THAT GIRL? YOU BETTER STOP IT OR...
S-STAY BACK OR I'LL TWIST HER NECK LIKE A...
GOOOMPH!
MY MOM TOLD ME TO ALWAYS PROTECT GIRLS FROM BULLIES.
SMAP
AWK!
WHO THE FUCK YOU THINK YOU ARE? I'LL SHOOT YOUR FUCKING HEAD OFF!
YOU HEAR THAT, ROY?
I'M AUTHORIZED TO PROTECT ALL MILITARY PERSONNEL IN ANY CIVIL DISPUTES, CORPORAL GEST.
BUZZZZIT
YOU OKAY, MA'AM?
YES. THANK YOU, I...
YOUR VOICE. IT SOUNDS... FAMILIAR.
YEAH.
YOURS DOES TOO.
BZZZZIT ZZITT
EEE! EEEE!
CLAP
CLAP CLAP
CLAP CLAP

EDGEFIELD, NEW JERSEY.
HONEEEY! I'M HOME!
HEY, BABE! IS THAT YOU?

A FEW YEARS FROM NOW.
IT WAS THE LAST TIME I CHECKED.
LOOK AT YOU. NO COAT. NO LUGGAGE.

I GOT EVERYTHING I NEED, RIGHT HERE.
YOU SMELL LIKE A STABLE.
HOW'D IT GO WITH THE MISSION OF MERCY?

ALLIE WASN'T TOO HARD TO TURN UP.
LAST I SAW OF HER IT LOOKED LIKE SHE WAS GONNA GO CRAWLING BACK TO HEALEY.
I KNOW YOU LIKE HER, BUT SHE IS SO PATHETIC.
I MEAN, HOW MANY TIMES DOES SOMEONE HAVE TO TRY SUICIDE?

SHE WENT THROUGH SOME REAL CHANGES THIS TIME AROUND.
BUT WHAT ABOUT YOU? ANYTHING GOIN' ON?
HMMM? ME? UMMM...

D'OH! I FORGOT TO SHOW YOU MY BIG SURPRISE DOWN CELLAR.
IT REALLY HAS BEEN AN EVENTFUL TRIP HOME.

NEEDHAWK AND BLANCHE!?
DID THESE HOPELESS FUCKS PULL SOME SHIT?
CREEPS WERE HIDING IN OUR CLOSET. TRIED TO JUMP AND PUMP ME.
AND YOU CLEANED THEIR CLOCKS? HAHAHA!
IT'S THE RANGER TRAINING. GIVES YOU A LOT OF HAND-TO-HAND EXPERIENCE, Y'KNOW?
IT JUST KICKS IN WHEN YOU NEED IT.
Mmmph
YOU AND BLANCHE NEVER DID UNDERSTAND HOW BUSINESS WORKS HERE IN EDGEFIELD, NEEDHAWK.
Mmmf mmmf
WHAT SAY WE GIVE 'EM A SHOW?
I'M KINKY. BUT NOT THAT KINKY.
Mmmf?
SO WHERE'S THE LINE, BABE? WILL I EVER KNOW JUST HOW FAR YOU'LL GO?
THINK OF IT AS A SEARCH IN PROGRESS.
I'LL TELL YOU WHEN WE FIND IT.
SO, UH... WHATEVER HAPPENED WITH YOU AND THAT MAGICIAN OF YOURS?
LAST TIME WE TALKED YOU WERE THINKIN' FLABBERGAST MIGHT BE MORE THAN JUST A TOY-BOY?
MORSE SAID HE TOOK OFF ON SOME MISSION OR MAGIC TOUR OR SOMETHING. IT WAS ALL KIND OF VAGUE.
YOU DIDN'T RUN INTO HIM OVER IN THE BAGH, DID YOU?

NAH.
NEVER LAID EYES ON HIM.
YEAH, WELL... BOTTOM LINE IS HE SPLIT AND NEVER BOTHERED TO CALL ME.
I KNOW WHAT THAT MEANS.
YOU'RE STUCK WITH ME, LOMAN! HAAHAHA!
HAHA BLUB!
YOU KNOW THAT SONG THAT EVERYONE'S GOT FOR THEIR RINGTONE?
YEAH.
WHENEVER I HEAR IT, YOU KNOW WHAT I SEE?
YOU AND ME. SETTIN' OUT FOR HEAVEN...
...IN OUR LITTLE SPEED BOAT.

A@L COMMAND FILES

EYES ONLY
Office of Motivation and Morale

RICK VEITCH (O-6, CO)

Rick Veitch is a lifelong cartoonist who was an early contributor to *Epic Illustrated* and *Heavy Metal* magazines. After collaborating with writer Alan Moore and inker Alfredo Alcala on the groundbreaking series SWAMP THING, Veitch both wrote and drew a long run on the title which can be found in the Vertigo collections SWAMP THING: REGENESIS, SWAMP THING: SPONTANEOUS GENERATION and SWAMP THING: INFERNAL TRIANGLES. He was also one of the founding artists on Moore's America's Best Comics line, cocreating Greyshirt for TOMORROW STORIES. The character was later spun off into the graphic novel GREYSHIRT: INDIGO SUNSET.

Veitch's most recent graphic novel, CAN'T GET NO, garnered fulsome critical praise and was named by *Publishers Weekly* as one of the best books of 2006. His other graphic novels include *Abraxas and the Earthman, Heartburst, The One, Brat Pack, The Maximortal, Rabid Eye, Pocket Universe* and *Crypto Zoo.*

Veitch is the cofounder, with Steve Conley, of the Internet comic site Comicon.com. He lives in Vermont with his wife Cindy and their two sons, Kirby and Ezra.

GARY ERSKINE (E-9, CSM)

Hailing from just outside Glasgow, Scotland, Gary Erskine began his comics career on *The Knights of Pendragon* and *Warheads* for Marvel UK. He went on to contribute artwork to the British anthology magazines *2000 AD* and *Crisis* (illustrating stories for such writers as Garth Ennis, Dan Abnett, Steve White and Michael Cook), and in 1993 he created the Tundra graphic novel *The Lords of Misrule* with writer John Tomlinson.

After working on various titles for DC, Dark Horse and Malibu through the 1990s (including STARMAN, *The Mask: World Tour, Terminator 2: Nuclear Twilight* and *Codename: Firearm*), in 2000 Erskine cocreated the critically acclaimed Image miniseries *City of Silence* with writer Warren Ellis. Since then he has also contributed to two of Garth Ennis's WAR STORIES – JOHANN'S TIGER and ARCHANGEL – as well as inking Chris Weston's pencils on the 13-issue Vertigo maxiseries THE FILTH, written by Grant Morrison.

Erskine is currently inking ARMY@LOVE and GREATEST HITS for Vertigo, as well as drawing covers for the Dark Horse miniseries *X-Wing: Rogue Leader*. He lives with his partner Mhairi in Glasgow and Heidelberg, Germany.

BRIAN K. VAUGHAN AND PIA GUERRA'S COMPELLING TALE OF THE LAST MAN ON EARTH UNFOLDS IN THESE COLLECTIONS FROM VERTIGO:

VERTIGO
BOOK 1

"This is why God created comic books."
— RevolutionSF.com

"This book blew us away."
— WIZARD

Brian K. Vaughan Pia Guerra José Marzán, Jr.

Y THE LAST MAN

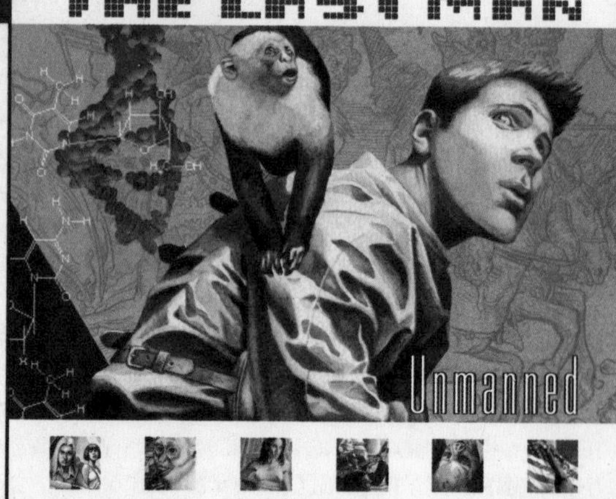

VOLUME 1: UNMANNED

ALSO AVAILABLE:
VOL. 2: CYCLES
VOL. 3: ONE SMALL STEP
VOL. 4: SAFEWORD
VOL. 5: RING OF TRUTH
VOL. 6: GIRL ON GIRL
VOL. 7: PAPER DOLLS

"COMPLETE AND UTTER COMIC GOLD."
— ***PUBLISHERS WEEKLY* (STARRED REVIEW)**

ALL TITLES ARE SUGGESTED FOR MATURE READERS.

SCI-FI ACTION COLLIDES WITH FAST-PACED DRAMA IN THIS EXPLOSIVE POLITICAL THRILLER FROM WRITER BRIAN K. VAUGHAN AND WILDSTORM:

EX MACHINA

VOLUME 1: THE FIRST HUNDRED DAYS

ALSO AVAILABLE:
VOL. 2: TAG
VOL. 3: FACT V. FICTION

"TERRIFICALLY INTRIGUING."
— ***ENTERTAINMENT WEEKLY***

SEARCH THE GRAPHIC NOVELS SECTION OF

www.VERTIGOCOMICS.com

FOR ART AND INFORMATION ON ALL OF OUR BOOKS!